Reaching Reluctant Young Adult Readers

A Handbook for Librarians and Teachers

Edward T. Sullivan

The Scarecrow Press, Inc.
Lanham, Maryland, and Oxford
2002

SCARECROW PRESS, INC.

Published in the United States of America
by Scarecrow Press, Inc.
A Member of the Rowman & Littlefield Publishing Group
4720 Boston Way, Lanham, Maryland 20706
www.scarecrowpress.com

PO Box 317
Oxford
OX2 9RU, UK

British Library Cataloguing in Publication Information Available

Library of Congress Cataloging-in-Publication Data Available

ISBN 0-8108-4343-9 (alk. paper)

∞™ The paper used in this publication meets the minimum requirements of American National Standard for Information Sciences—Permanence of Paper for Printed Library Materials, ANSI/NISO Z39.48-1992.
Manufactured in the United States of America.

Contents

Introduction

"I *hate* to read." I have lost count of how many times I have heard these words spoken by a young adult. It is just as well because it would be far too depressing to contemplate the numbers. Those words are what I inevitably hear every time I walk into middle and high school classrooms to talk to students about the public library. They always seem to come from the mouth of a boy, and he always speaks those words with a grin of defiant pride on his face. The boy is never alone. His remarks are always followed with approving laughter from his classmates (usually other boys), who share his disdain for reading. Girls seem to know better. There are plenty of them who hate to read too, but they are smart enough to know that it is nothing of which to be proud. Those words never cease to break my heart but, of course, I always try to think of a snappy comeback like "Oh, well you just haven't found the right book yet." My hope is that they will indeed do just that, but it is hard to be optimistic when you hear those words come from the mouth of a sixth, seventh, or eighth grader. It's downright depressing to hear such sentiments expressed by a junior or senior in high school because I know they are already at the point of no return. If they hate to read at that late stage in life, what is it going to take to get them to love it? I also have to wonder how those kids end up that way. Who and/or what is responsible for turning them off to reading, assuming they were ever turned on? Those kids have been failed by their parents, by their teachers, and by their public libraries.

So much has been written about the problem of illiteracy. Tens of millions of people in the United States alone cannot read or write. Globally, the problem is even more severe. It is indeed a horrendous problem that, if not properly addressed and resolved, will have dire consequences for everyone's quality of life everywhere. Fortunately, illiteracy is a problem that does receive a great deal of attention (albeit not all it deserves), and is addressed through a variety of programs in both the private and public sectors.

As urgent a problem as illiteracy is, however, a more significant problem affecting our society that receives little attention and is rarely addressed by our education or public library systems is *aliteracy*, which is best defined as a condition in which one can read but chooses not to.

1

People with this problem are often referred to as nonreaders or reluctant readers. Aliteracy is as rampant among young adults as it is among adults and children. My concern here, however, is with young adults. If aliteracy is a problem affecting people of all ages, why focus on young adults? That audience is the focus of discussion in this book because it is in the early young adult years that there is one last opportunity to turn these kids away from aliteracy and lead them to become lifelong readers.

Before going any further, it is necessary to define what I mean by "young adult." The Young Adult Library Services Association defines a young adult as anyone between the ages of twelve and eighteen. That definition is generally accepted among the library and teaching professions, and in the publishing industry. I, however, am going to stretch that range a bit. For the purposes of my discussions, I am going to define a young adult as anyone between the ages of ten and fifteen. For teachers' point of reference, that age range will include fifth through ninth grades.

There are several reasons for my taking liberties with the traditional definition of young adult. I include ten and eleven-year-olds because they are stuck in a kind of "no man's land" when it comes to library services. As public library children's services have moved down to serve the youngest, older children have been left grossly underserved. Although there is plenty in a children's collection a ten or eleven-year-old would find enjoyable and challenging, little attention or effort is typically given to programming for or serving the needs of these ages. The emphasis is placed upon the very young, often only on the pre-literate. Even if children's departments did give older children more attention, I don't think it would make them any more inclined to make use of the library. Ten and eleven-year-olds, who are sometimes referred to as "tweens," really want nothing to do with a children's room. They consider themselves too old for "kid stuff." They do not want to be considered children any longer and so will not take advantage of children's services or use the collections. What children at that age do want, if they do read, are young adult books and to attend young adult programs. They are closer to being teens than children and want to associate themselves with books and programs for teens. That being the case, it seems only logical to include them here.

Another reason for including ten and eleven-year-olds in these discussions is because it is at this age that aliteracy becomes a significant problem. Bernice Cullinan goes so far as to say that this age "is a period for a last ditch effort to turn children into readers" (124). Hollis Lowery-Moore notes: "Test scores and reading surveys indicate that many middle school/junior high students hit an academic slump somewhere between the fifth and eighth grades" (24). Arthea Reed also offers some insight into why the middle school years are a critical time for reading habits:

> The peak of reading interest often occurs around age twelve; that is also the age when many readers lose interest in books. This happens for several reasons. Young readers are required by schools or pushed by parents to read books for which they are not emotionally and intellectually ready. Many young adults have difficulty finding books with young characters who face the problems of adolescence. Conversely, adolescents are gaining emotional and intellectual maturity, but the books they are reading are not keeping up with their maturity, and they do not know how to locate more appropriate books. Many parents, teachers, and librarians are unaware of appropriate books to recommend. Some adults discourage adolescents from selecting books on certain topics or themes of interest. For some adolescents, reading is not accepted by their peer group. (26-27)

Reed cites a host of factors contributing to why students in the middle school years "drop out" and "turn off" to reading. One of the most significant factors she cites is the adults in these young people's lives. Librarians, parents, and teachers do indeed all share complicity in turning many kids *off* to reading and *on* to lifelong aliteracy. That is an issue that will be explored at great length in this book. There are some other factors to consider as well. It is in these middle school years that boys and girls become involved with many things that can distract them from reading: computer and video games, extracurricular activities, the Internet, sports, and unsupervised television viewing are just a few. By early adolescence, young people find themselves preoccupied with a virtually all-consuming distraction called puberty.

If these young people on the brink of adolescence or already engaged in the early stages of it are not already firmly established as enthusiastic, lifelong readers, then this is the last chance librarians and teachers have to take them down that road. If we miss this final opportunity to turn them on to reading, then they are doomed to live their lives as aliterates.

Does that mean it's too late for high school students? Many people will disagree with me, but I believe it is. By ninth or tenth grade, educational foundations are well established. A teen who has been a nonreader all of the preceding years is not likely to change his or her ways. Kimberly Leanne Collins, a voracious reader, speaks to this idea when she says:

> It doesn't matter if the book is school related or not, I'm happy just as long as I'm reading. My passion is reading. I love to read, anything and anywhere. Ever since I can remember, I've had a book in my hand. I'm seventeen now and a senior in high school. When I'm not reading for course requirements, I read what I like. (1)

The genuine passion this teenager has for reading is the culmination of a lifetime experience she has had with books and reading that goes back as far as she can remember. There is little a librarian or teacher can do, at that late stage of life, to turn a teenager on to reading. I base that belief on my experience teaching high school, and university undergraduate and graduate students, and working as a young adult librarian.

The purpose of this book is to offer resources and strategies librarians and teachers can use to get kids into the habit of reading before they reach the point of no return. That is why the focus here is on "tweens" and young teens, those students in the middle school years of their education who are most at-risk with reading.

It is important to remember that this book is not addressing reading disabilities or the problems non-native English speakers have with reading. This book is only about those kids who have the ability to read, who have been taught the basic skills needed to read, but do not.

This book is intended to be a practical tool for librarians and teachers to use. To that end, I have assembled here the information and tools necessary to fight aliteracy. The book begins with a chapter defining what aliteracy is, and its causes and effects. That is followed with a discussion of what strategies you can utilize to entice aliterates to read.

It is necessary to define the disease and its symptoms before pursuing a cure. The rest of the book will focus on resources, the various materials you can use try to turn kids on to reading. You will find these chapters to be much more than a series of bibliographies and lists. There is also discussion of how these materials can be used specifically with aliterates. The book does discuss research and theory, but that information is presented in a practical context that educators can use and apply to their own individual situations. Consider this book a guide to everything you need to confront and combat aliteracy.

Works Cited

Collins, Kimberly Leanne. "Litanies of a Literature Lover, or Confessions of a Young Adult Reader." *Mosaics of Meaning Enhancing the Intellectual Life of Young Adults through Story.* Ed. Kay E. Vandergrift. Lanham, MD: Scarecrow, 1996.

Cullinan, Bernice E. *Read to Me: Raising Kids Who Love to Read.* New York: Scholastic, 1992.

Lowery-Moore, Hollis. "Voices of Middle School Readers." *Into Focus: Understanding and Creating Middle School Readers.* Eds.

Kylene Beers and Barbara G. Samuels. Norwood, MA: Christopher-Gordon, 1998.

Reed, Arthea J. S. *Comics to Classics: A Guide to Books for Teens and Preteens.* New York: Penguin, 1994.

Chapter 1
Aliteracy and the Reluctant Reader

In this chapter, research from the related fields of English education, reading education, and library science is focused on these critical questions: What is aliteracy? What are reluctant readers? How can reluctant readers be identified? What are some of the causes of aliteracy? The answers to these questions will provide the fundamental knowledge needed to articulate goals and strategies for attacking the aliteracy problem.

Defining the Problem

Reluctant readers are not the same as poor readers, that is, students who possess some sort of reading disability, or are lacking in developmental foundations or mechanical skills. On the contrary, reluctant readers are perfectly able to read but do not. As Patrick Jones succinctly puts it: "Reluctant readers are not stupid; they are kids who do not choose to read" (168). Aidan Chambers defines reluctant readers as those students "who have the ability to read without any mechanical problems but have little or no inclination to except what is required by way of work or normal everyday life" (4). Mary Lenox concurs with Chambers's definition but also adds that this lack of motivation is likely to produce a permanent nonreading habit (353). If, after finishing school, such students find themselves in a situation where reading is not a necessity, they will simply not read at all. This nonreading condition has been labeled *aliteracy*, a term first coined by Larry Mikulecky to identify those who can read but do not.

Kylene Beers (1990) takes issue with this term. She notes: "The word literally means without, or lacking, literacy. . . . A student called aliterate, then, would be one lacking in some dimension of literacy; however, this may not be true. One could be literate at all levels and still choose not to be a reader. Not reading does not necessarily imply not being literate" (11). Beers's point is well taken. It is important to always remember that aliterates, reluctant readers, can indeed read. Arthea Reed points out that "often we confuse reluctance with inability

7

to read" (33). Reluctant readers do have at least skills to read on a basic level, but their lack of reading practice prevents them developing fluency in the skill. Lack of motivation should not be confused with inability, but librarians and teachers should be careful to not presume too much ability. The term aliteracy has been generally accepted as Mikulecky defines it. In addition to the term *reluctant reader*, aliterates have also been labeled *nonreaders*, *unmotivated readers*, and *literate nonreaders*. Reluctant reader, however, is the most widely used of those terms. For purposes of discussion here, I am using the terms aliterate and reluctant reader interchangeably.

Identifying Reluctant Readers

In her research with seventh grade students, Beers (1996) identifies three distinct voices among aliterates, which she labels as *dormant*, *uncommitted*, and *unmotivated*. Dormant readers are those students who like to read but do not make the time to do it. Beers finds that these readers do possess positive attitudes toward reading, shaped by memories of their parents reading to them on a regular basis, having their own books at home, and having experiences which impressed upon them that reading books was an enjoyable activity. Uncommitted and unmotivated readers, however, have no such positive regard for reading. Beers notes that these students lack any early immersion into literature. These students recalled few times, if any, when parents read to them. This type of reader reads efferently. They have no aesthetic appreciation of the reading experience (111). Indeed, Beers finds in her research "that the less a student liked to read, the more he or she viewed it as a skill" (32). Uncommitted readers are able to envision themselves as eventually becoming good readers and also look positively upon people who do enjoy reading. Although they do share with uncommitted readers the view of reading as only a skill, unmotivated readers differ in that they express negative feelings toward people who enjoy reading and could also not see themselves reading in the future (33).

Although generalization is never a good thing, there are certain characteristics that have been consistently observed among many reluctant readers. Lance Gentile and Merna McMillan cite ten common factors contributing to the making of a reluctant reader:

1. By the time many students reach high school, they equate reading with ridicule, failure, or exclusively school-related tasks.

2. Students are not excited by ideas. They prefer to experience life directly rather than through reading.
3. Many active adolescents are unable to sit still long enough to read for any prolonged period of time.
4. Teenagers are too self-absorbed and preoccupied with themselves, their problems, families, sexual roles, etc., to make connections between their world and books.
5. Books are inadequate entertainment compared to other competing media such as television, video games, and the Internet.
6. Persistent stress from home and school to read constantly is counterproductive for some adolescents.
7. Adolescents may grow up in nonreading homes void of reading material with no reading role models. There is no one to pass down the value of reading.
8. Some adolescents may consider reading solitary and anti-social.
9. Reading is considered "uncool," and something adults do.
10. Some adolescents view reading as part of the adult world and reject it outright. (650-653)

Knowing some of the common factors contributing to aliteracy will help professionals recognize teens who have an aversion to reading and are in need of help.

Why Aliteracy Is a Problem

If aliterates are capable of reading, if they do have the basic skills to read, then why be concerned about whether they exercise these skills? After all, reluctant readers can read if they have to, and they will read to function. Incredible as it may seem, I have encountered many teachers (many of them reading teachers, no less!) who actually subscribe to this absurd notion. Perhaps there may even be people reading this book who believe it too. Just in case there are, let me put to rest any impression you may have that aliteracy is anything less than an urgent crisis in our society. William J. Baroody offers the best explanation for why aliteracy is a deeply serious problem that cannot be ignored.

> Aliteracy reflects a change in cultural values and a loss of skills, both of which threaten the processes of a free and democratic society. Literacy . . . knits people together, giving them a common culture . . . and provides people with the

>intellectual tools used to question, challenge, understand,
>disagree, and arrive at consensus . . . it allows people to
>participate in an exchange of ideas. . . . Aliteracy leads
>inexorably to a two-tiered society: the knowledgeable elite and
>the masses. It makes a common culture illusory or impossible;
>it erodes the basis for effective decision making and
>participation in the democratic process. (ix)

Baroody is not exaggerating when he cites aliteracy as a threat to the democratic process. After all, what good is knowing how to read if you do not do it? An open and free society must be an informed and enlightened one, and it cannot be if its citizens do not read. G. Robert Carlsen notes: "One of the important criteria in judging a nation is the percent of its people who *can* read. And one of the important criteria in judging an individual's cultural level is whether he *does* read" (2). Frank Smith describes the problem of aliteracy as "one of the great tragedies of contemporary education," explaining that "many students . . . graduate with an antipathy to reading . . . despite the abilities they might have." (177) Let us also not forget that reading is not just about information. Yes, we read to stay informed, but reading also makes us more human. As Carlsen eloquently says: "Reading expands life. The reader comes to know life in other parts of the world and in other periods of history. He knows something of the range of human existence" (1). Young people will never know any of that if the only impression they have of reading is that it is void of pleasure, nothing more than a bunch of skills, drills, worksheets, and standardized tests. Unfortunately, that is the depth to which reading education has sunk.

Factors Contributing to Aliteracy

Educators

There is no question that teachers share a great deal of the blame in turning adolescents away from reading. Reading education focuses entirely on teaching students the mechanics of reading. Students learn how to decode and perhaps comprehend, but they are rarely taught more than those basic skills. With all of the emphasis placed on teaching skills, students are never given the opportunity to experience the pleasures of reading. As Barbara Decker observes:

>If reading instruction for children comes exclusively from a
>vocabulary-controlled reader, ditto sheet skill drills, and
>workbooks, then students are not likely to learn that reading

can be pleasurable and exciting. If children are tested on their knowledge of discrete skills instead of their ability to comprehend what they read, then they will be taught these skills in isolation . . . Furthermore, over-emphasis on teaching decoding and structural analysis skills in order to pass a state mandated skills test requires that instructional time be spent teaching the student test taking skills as well. Consequently, the joy of reading is never discovered, for there is not time left for the reading activities that lead to a true literacy. (56)

To be fair to classroom teachers, they may want to do more but are increasingly put in a position in which they cannot.

The latest raging fad in education is accountability and standards (as if those concepts never before existed in education), which mean endless batteries of standardized tests to measure students' ability and gauge teachers' success or failure in instilling basic skills. Consequences for students "failing" such tests are absurd. They are held back from moving to the next grade level. Their schools can be put on probation, and their teachers and principals can be demoted or fired. What is created, then, is an environment of anxiety and fear with teachers, fearing reprisals from their superiors, and forced to reduce reading education to the superficial level found in these tests. Students, who certainly do not need more pressure added to their already anxiety-filled lives, are told that the reputation of their school rests upon their shoulders. Worse is the attitude this approach instills in students toward reading. Alice Winkle observes that: "While high achievement scores on standardized tests are viewed by the schools and by the public as proof of successful instructional programs, many students find little or no pleasure in reading when it is presented as a series of skill and drill lessons year after year" (43). The result of all this is that students are taught the "basic skills" of reading, so they can successfully pass the test and meet "standards," but never progress beyond that foundation because there is no time for advancement.

There is also a problem with how students are taught to interact with literature in the classroom. Louise Rosenblatt, a proponent of the "transactional theory" of reading, explains that readers can approach reading in one of two ways: aesthetic or efferent. Students who read efferently are "focused primarily on what will remain as the residue after the reading," while those students who read aesthetically will be concerned "with what happens during the actual reading event" (24). It is the efferent approach to reading, the less desirable of the two in terms of instilling any joy for reading, that teachers typically impress upon their students. Too many teachers do not see as one of their roles instilling in their students an appreciation for literature. They have a rigid utilitarian view toward books. They look at how a book can be "used." "What kind of lessons can I pull from this book?" "How does this book relate to the curriculum?" Those are the kinds of questions teachers ask themselves about books. To them, books and the reading of them are a means rather than an end. A book is simply another tool to be used in the classroom to teach the lesson. Granted, teachers do have to consider such things. That is their job, what they are expected to do. But is that all? Should they not also concern themselves with exciting their students about reading so that they will pursue it with enthusiasm inside and outside of the classroom, and for the rest of their lives? Instilling an appreciation and love for reading, and developing critical and analytical skills may indeed be one of the ultimate goals of educators, but how often do such goals come even close to being addressed when reading is invariably reduced to book reports offering plot summaries, daily quizzes, and vocabulary tests?

What a colossal waste it is when the reading experience culminates in taking the Accelerated Reader® test, as it does in thousands of schools these days. Opportunities are rarely given for students to discuss what it is they are reading. They do not have the chance to reflect upon or think critically about what they read. A personal connection a student can make with a text through discussion with the teacher and fellow classmates is denied. What time can be devoted to that pursuit is instead wasted upon lectures in which the teacher tells the student what to think about the text and upon quizzes and vocabulary drills which contribute absolutely nothing to enhancing the students' reading experience. Jody Podl notes: "Even capable students' confidence can be destroyed by quizzes filled with arcane details, lectures that elucidate the absolute 'truth' of the literature, and tests that require regurgitating these truths rather than making personal connections" (56). Taught as it is now in most schools, reading to many students is not a pleasure to anticipate, but a drudgery to dread.

Instilled with a negative perception of "reading as drudgery" in the elementary school years, what happens to students in the middle and high school years? Bernice Cullinan suggests this consequence:

> Some say that if children are not readers by the time they leave elementary school, they probably will never become active readers. I don't exactly agree with this dire prediction but I will say that if children never read or hear a really *good* book by the time they are teenagers, they are not likely to become readers. (124)

I believe the prediction is worse than Cullinan may be willing to admit. The negative perceptions of reading cultivated in the elementary grades are too often reinforced in the middle and high school years. The act of reading itself is certainly treated no differently, if not worse. Students are still forced to answer superficial questions in ridiculous quizzes and worksheets, and to complete more vocabulary drills. To compound the problem, students are required to read books in which they have no interest. John Bushman conducted a study on what, if any, young adult literature was being used in sixth through twelfth grade classrooms. Bushman found that sixth and seventh graders were most likely to read young adult literature as assigned reading, but classics reigned supreme in grades eight through twelve. He says, "With few exceptions, teachers assigned classics for students to read as in-class reading. What was more disturbing to me were the actual titles that students had to read. What was once considered literature for grades eleven and twelve has now filtered down to grades eight, nine, and ten" (36). Young adult author Walter Dean Myers raises another important issue that seldom comes up in research about aliteracy and reluctant readers. He asks if the reason that Asian, Black, or Latino students may resist reading could be related to the fact that they are not given the opportunity to read literature that has characters or situations with which they can identify (15). Myers raises the important point that one way to get reluctant readers to read is to make available to them books which are culturally relevant to them.

Not only are students asked to read books that have little to which they can relate, it is also literature, which they are not intellectually prepared to appreciate or fathom. As Jim Cope (1997), a professor of English education, observes, "Before students can effectively analyze a text, they must be able to make a personal response to it" (20). Bushman was also disturbed to find that "the number of books students read decreased as they moved from freshman to senior year." He observes, "Teachers don't seem to care if students continue to read or not. They have done what is expected of them (pass along a cultural/literary heritage), and making young people lifelong readers is not a part of the plan" (38). Cope (1997) expresses a similar sentiment:

> One of the most common arguments for using classics in middle and high school classrooms is that we want to challenge our students. By pushing them to analyze literature that they are not developmentally ready for, we believe we will somehow instill a passion for the great works. What happens instead is that we extinguish any love for literature that might already be there. Despite clear signs of student

apathy and nonlearning, we too often resolutely trudge
onward. (20)

As a former teacher of English literature, I certainly cannot argue with
the desire to expose students to the glorious musings of such authors as
Chaucer and Shakespeare. But to what end must that be done? Must it
be done to the point that, after having *Julius Caesar* and *The
Canterbury Tales* forced down their throats, students are left with a
permanent distaste for reading?

I never cease to be amazed at the attitude so many middle and high
school teachers hold toward young adult literature. Many view it as
sub-literature, not worthy of serious consideration or study. Aside from
the one token course in adolescent literature they may be required to
take for secondary teacher certification, many teachers graduate from
teacher education programs virtually ignorant of the canon of young
adult literature that has been growing for thirty-plus years, a canon
containing thousands of works that are as deep and compelling as any
so-called classic. Secondary teachers are not alone. I consistently find
many elementary teachers completely ignorant of children's literature.
Imagine third graders assigned to read titles like *The Adventures of Tom
Sawyer*, *Little Women*, and *The Man in the Iron Mask*. That is an actual
school assignment I encountered in the public library.

Teachers cannot entirely be blamed for this ignorance. In order to
be a secondary teacher of English, one must be an English major. I
challenge anyone to find a course in children's or young adult literature
taught as part of an English department curriculum. My undergraduate
alma mater did offer a course called "adolescent literature," but S. E.
Hinton was the only bona fide young adult author taught in the course.
Other selections taught included Henry Roth's *Call It Sleep*, Harper
Lee's *To Kill a Mockingbird*, and J. D. Salinger's *The Catcher in the
Rye*. Granted, all of these books have adolescent protagonists and
marginal teen appeal, but they were written for adults, not teenagers,
and that makes a world of difference. They may indeed be books that
will appeal to some young adult readers, but they are not young adult
books. The disdain teachers have for young adult literature is instilled
in them by their English professors. "Kiddie lit" is not worthy of
serious academic consideration.

Good intentions may indeed be the motivation for teachers force
feeding classics to their students, but they are only succeeding in
turning them off completely to reading for pleasure. Would it really be
so tragic if a student graduated from high school never having read *The
Scarlet Letter* or a Shakespeare play? Will he or she be incapable of
leading a full, productive life? My contention is that the real concern of

teachers is not to graduate students who are lifelong lovers of reading, but rather ingrain in them their own or their school's cultural literacy agenda. What damage is done to students in the course of that indoctrination is of little concern. Concluding his study of middle and high school language arts curriculums, John Bushman observes:

> It seems that schools have accomplished just the opposite of what they intend to do: they have turned students off from reading rather than making them lifelong readers. Schools have failed to choose literature that enables students to become emotionally and cognitively involved in what they read. If students are asked to read literature that is not consistent with their developmental levels, they will not be able to interact fully with that literature. As a result, students who do not interact with the literature are left with learning only about the literature—information that works well on the television program *Jeopardy*, but that does not help students connect the text with their goals, level of development, and experience. (38)

Forcing students to read books that are "for their own good" will leave them with a resentment for reading so profound that they may leave high school, college bound or not, regarding reading for enjoyment or personal enlightenment as a completely alien concept. Mary Leonhardt, a veteran classroom teacher, observes: "Currently, only assigned reading is respected, which is ironic because assigned reading at a K-12 level is fraught with problems. It drives out the pleasure of reading, for one thing, and drives out reading altogether" (30). Cope (1998) concurs:

> I can report that a majority of our best students enter college viewing literature with the same excitement as they would a Lawrence Welk marathon. . . .with few exceptions, adolescent literature is absent from their English classes. And students are paying the price. Being forced to read so-called "great literature" (the "classics") before they are ready for it has taught them that literature is something to be endured and almost never enjoyed. (9)

A lack of motivation is only part of the damage done to students who have not had the opportunity to read adolescent literature in school. The vitally important analytical and critical thinking skills that develop from engaging relevant, quality literature are grossly underdeveloped. Cope (1998) observes:

> Lack of experience with literature that is both well written and developmentally appropriate causes them to read literature like they would a newspaper. They search for important facts that they can regurgitate on tests so that they can get through the last literature class they will ever have to take. They are almost never moved by what they read. They rarely incorporate the characters' experiences and discoveries into their own hearts or minds. They don't believe those who tell them that they are missing something. They don't understand that what they are missing is important, vital, maybe even essential. (9)

That is why I constantly encounter students coming into the library looking for the *Cliffs Notes* for a particular title or asking if there is a movie version. Who can blame them? These students are just reacting to what they have been taught over the years, that reading is not a meaningful experience. There is nothing more to get out of reading than what *Cliffs Notes* has conveniently boiled down in his concise "guide," so why not just skip the actual book and go straight to him? Leonhardt writes of the same problem:

> By high school, this practice is endemic to students. Just the fact that a book is assigned makes it unappealing to kids, and they become very streetwise about ways to avoid reading it. They rent the movie, read the *Cliff's Notes*, or just ask their more conscientious friends what the book is about. (30)

That is the lesson students are learning in classrooms these days, and it is a tragic one.

School Libraries

The problem is not only in the classroom, but also in the school library. Ideally, every school should have a fully functioning library stocked with current age-appropriate books, periodicals, and reference tools, and equipped with current, relevant information technologies. The facility should be run by a professional (i.e., degreed and trained) librarian, who knows the literature and the technology, and who can advise and instruct students and teachers in how to most effectively use it in the curriculum. In short, the school library (or media center, if you must) should be the backbone of curricular support. Beyond that utilitarian definition, the school library should also be a place where students can get excited about reading. It should be a place where students come to find information not only because they have to, but also because they want to. Judith Davidson and David Koppenhaver observe:

> Excellent classroom, school, and public library collections are important resources for supporting reading habits. Strong fiction and nonfiction collections encourage young people to turn to literacy as an essential tool for learning, from reading for pleasure and gathering information to exploring new curriculum topics and investigating questions of concern. (24)

The school library should be a place that stimulates and feeds curiosity and imagination for its own sake, and that stimulation can be fostered only through a properly equipped and staffed facility.

The reality is that most school libraries do not even come close to meeting that ideal. Now that computer technologies and the Internet are the current bandwagons for educators, school libraries are being transformed into high-tech computer labs, which would be all well and good were it not for the fact that these technologies are often purchased at the expense of books. As school libraries are having personal computers and high speed Internet connections installed, moldy books that are completely obsolete can be found collecting another layer of dust on the shelves. In the library I recently inherited in east Tennessee, I had to weed all of the country books because they had an average copyright date of 1973. In middle school libraries throughout Staten Island, I found books on shelves about space exploration that pre-date the first moon landing, or Sputnik. There are books about drugs that make no mention of crack or a "designer drug," like Ecstasy because they did not exist at the time of publication. There are books about countries that no longer exist, like the Soviet Union, East and West Germany, and Yugoslavia. There are books about African and Asian countries written in the 1950s that are blatantly racist. Books on health and the sciences have publication dates going back thirty years or more. On the shelf of one middle school library, I found a biography of Dwight Eisenhower written while he was serving his first term as President. Novels in the collection had copyright dates going back to the 1950s. There may be a set of encyclopedias that are current enough to be useful, but most other reference books are hopelessly outdated. For periodicals, there may be three or four subscriptions to weekly news magazines or *National Geographic*.

Even if these libraries were actually staffed by a professional librarian (most are not), they would not be able to do much about the problem anyway. New York state law requires school libraries to have so many volumes on their shelves. Of course, the law makes no mention of the currency or quality of those volumes. That's why schools can keep completely irrelevant, obsolete books on their library shelves and get away with it. Principals, who typically have no clue as to what a school library should be, usually have discretion on how to distribute their budget and, of course, the library is inevitably their lowest priority. I have been in some schools where principals have converted libraries to extra classrooms, office space, or storage rooms. And yet they shake their heads in astonishment at how low their students score on reading tests. In 1990, Jack Humphrey found that:

> The average school library is adding less than one-half book per student each year. Assuming that this number has been added each year for the past 10 years, a school with 500 students would have purchased about 2,500 books. There may be 10,000 books in the library, but many of the 7,500 books purchased over 10 years ago may be of little value to students. (94)

Over ten years later, the trend Humphrey cites continues and has, from what I have observed, worsened. The problem with school libraries is not confined to Staten Island or New York City. It is a nationwide problem that seems particularly acute in large cities like Chicago, New York, and Philadelphia, and it is endemic to the aliteracy problem now rampant among adolescents.

Public Libraries

Public libraries also often share complicity in doing little or nothing to get and keep teens excited about reading. Most public libraries have some kind of active service to children, particularly younger children, regularly offering read aloud and storytelling programs and other activities to promote literacy. Discussing the implications for public libraries of survey results from the National Center for Education Statistics, Mary K. Chelton notes: "Eighty-six percent of libraries offer group programs for preschool and kindergarten-age children" (104). For older children, however, there is progressively less programming. By the time children reach fifth or sixth grade, there is usually, other than summer reading programs, nothing being offered by their public libraries to promote recreational reading. Age-appropriate books are available for them to read, but there is little effort on the part of the library to encourage the reading of those books. Other than afterschool reference service, there is little the public library offers to older elementary age children. This is puzzling because many of these same libraries typically do a fine job of aggressively promoting literacy development among preschool and primary school age children through frequent, regular programming and other initiatives. It is as if there is a belief that, by the time children have reached fourth grade, their literacy development has been achieved and there is no longer a need to promote it. I can see this very attitude prevail among the schools I work with in Staten Island. They are very good about bringing kindergarten through third grade classes regularly to the public library for browsing and reading aloud, but this activity suddenly ceases in fourth grade. Is there a presumption that children have suddenly been transformed into literate readers when they graduate from third grade? So it would seem. That is, of course, utter nonsense. At that age, assuming all things are equal, children are just beginning to form a solid foundation in literacy. To suddenly cease virtually all efforts to strengthen and build upon that foundation is detrimental to further development.

What further compounds this problem is the progressive lack of public library service offered to adolescents. Services for teenagers, other than reference help, in many, if not most, public libraries are nonexistent. Few public libraries, regardless of size, employ a professional designated as a young adult librarian or a teen specialist. According to Chelton: "Only 52 percent of public libraries report employing a librarian specifically trained to work with children or young adults; 39 percent of those libraries employ a children's librarian; 11 percent a young adult librarian; and 24 percent a youth services specialist" (106). Services to adolescents are often left to the department or librarian designated with the more generic "youth services" title, but that position is typically expected to serve both children *and* teenagers, an impossible task. To seriously expect an individual or even a department to serve both audiences properly is absurd. In such situations, the youth services person or people have to decide whom to focus on, and it is inevitably the older children and teens who lose. Even if the young adult books are kept, as they always should be, separate from the adult and children's collections, no one is available to market the collection to teens. Chelton observes that 58 percent of public libraries maintain a separate young adult section, which is down from 84 percent of public libraries reporting such sections in 1988 (108). Another troubling fact to consider is that if only 11 percent of public libraries are employing a young adult specialist, who is doing the selecting, maintaining, and promoting for the libraries that do have separate young adult collections? That responsibility is inevitably falling upon someone who, however well intentioned, does not have knowledge, skills, or time to give the job the attention it requires and deserves. Public libraries are doing the right thing maintaining separate young adult sections, but there needs to be a professional on staff to consistently promote these books to teens. Lack of sufficient budget and personnel are two of the reasons administrators cite for the absence of specialized staff, inadequate collections, and programming for adolescents. Not allocating a separate area for young adult materials is attributed to lack of space. Of course, it is true that public libraries are inadequately funded and staffed, and find themselves cramped for shelf space as they must adapt to new formats and technologies. It is telling, however, that of all the services a library offers, it is the service to young adults that typically falls victim first to these burdens. The fact is that service to adolescents is not a priority among many public libraries. Young adults comprise as much as one third of the total number of patrons using the library, but that age group is the recipient of a grossly disproportionate piece of the budget when it comes to purchasing materials, hiring staff, and implementing other services directly benefiting their needs. The low priority given to young adult services can be dressed up in talk about inadequate budgeting and space and staff shortages, but the cause is really rooted in the prejudice many adults have toward teenagers. The awful truth is often that they simply do not want teenagers in the library, and they do all they can to make the most unappealing, unwelcoming environment possible. One of the most significant consequences of this prejudice is millions of adolescents growing up into adults who hate to read because the public libraries in their communities cannot be bothered to serve them.

Parents

Parents also share some of the blame, not so much in turning kids off to reading, but rather in never turning them on to it in the first place. I have yet to encounter in the public library a child (accompanied by a parent) who is not a genius. This is, of course, the parent's perception, not the child's. Their daughters or sons always read far beyond grade level (whatever that means), so they must read something more complex than what the children choose for themselves. I consistently see this happening not only with young children, but with middle and high school-age teens as well. Parents disparage their child's preference for *Animorphs*, *Buffy the Vampire Slayer*, *Fear Street*, *Goosebumps*, *Sweet Valley* because they view such books as "trash," subliterature not worthy of their genius children's time. Never mind the fact that that is what they *want* to read. Reading series books are exactly what many young people need to become comfortable with and confident in their reading. Parents forcing their children to read books for which they are not developmentally prepared and not interested in reading serves no purpose other than to reinforce what they are already learning in school: reading sucks. An argument can be made that these parents are bringing their kids to the library to check out books (never mind what irreparable harm they are causing them while there) is better than the alternative of not bringing them at all. At least those parents, misguided as they are, recognize that reading is important and are making some effort to get their kids to do it.

Over the years, research has shown again and again that children who grow up with nonreading parents in a home that is devoid of reading materials are much more likely to grow up aliterate. An early study by O'Rourke states that "parental reading habits are a major influence on the reading habits of their children" (340). Leonhardt (1995) plainly says, "it's undeniable that children raised in homes without books, and without parents who love reading, are at a great disadvantage" (24). Beers (1998) also discusses the importance of these formative years in her study of adolescents who choose not to read:

> The contrast between parents of children who have positive attitudes toward reading and those with negative attitudes is obvious. Children with positive attitudes toward reading had parents who spent a lot of time firmly planting the notion that reading is an enjoyable, worthwhile activity. Most of these parents were creating for their children, without even realizing it, an aesthetic stance toward reading. Though this took a lot of time on their part, it was time well spent. (52)

Before a child even begins attending school, in some of their most formative years, parents have an important and unique opportunity to impress upon their children a love of reading.

Many parents do not read aloud to their children, or play rhyming or singing games with them. They do not buy books for their children or take them to the public library. Most important, they do not present themselves as reading role models for their children by reading in front of them. Children want to do the things they see their parents doing. If they see their parents reading, they will want to read, too. If they see their parents reading with enjoyment and enthusiasm, they are likely to appreciate it, too.

There is an initiative in the New York City public school system called Project Read, which identifies children in the younger elementary grades who are "at risk" for reading problems and offers afterschool enrichment for these students. There are also workshops and other activities for the parents of these children and in my work with the New York Public Library I have had the opportunity to speak to many of these parents' groups. Not surprisingly, the parents of these children in Project Read are not avid readers themselves. What astonishes me is the inability of parents to understand the connection between their nonreading to their child's. They do not recognize the importance of reading to their children every day, of presenting themselves as reading role models to their children, of having lots of different kinds of reading materials in their home to inspire curiosity in their children, or buying books for their children instead of the latest video game.

To be fair to these parents, their inability to grasp the problems and to embrace the solutions is rooted in their own childhood experiences. The parents of these children did not grow up in homes full of reading materials with parents who read to them or for themselves. They did not grow up regularly visiting their local public library. They were not educated in schools that instilled in them the joy of reading.

Aliteracy is a vicious cycle. These parents who were failed by their own parents, public libraries, and schools, cannot pass on to their children what they never knew. What we, as librarians and teachers, have to do is try to find ways of breaking this vicious cycle. In the next chapter and those that follow are discussions of the many strategies and resources we can use to do just that.

Works Cited

Baroody, William J. "Foreword." *Aliteracy: People Who Can Read but Won't*. Washington, D. C.: American Enterprise Institute for Public Policy Research, 1984.

Beers, G. Kylene. *Choosing Not to Read: An Ethnographic Study of Seventh-Grade Aliterate Readers*. Unpublished Doctoral Dissertation. University of Houston, 1990.

―――. "Choosing Not to Read: Understanding Why Some Middle Schoolers Just Say No." *Into Focus: Understanding and Creating Middle School Readers*. Eds. Kylene Beers and Barbara G. Daniels. Norwood, MA: Christopher-Gordon, 1998.

————. "No Time, No Interest, No Way! Three Voices of Aliteracy." *School Library Journal* (February 1996): 30-33.

————. "No Time, No Interest, No Way! Part 2." *School Library Journal* (March 1996): 110-113.

Bushman, John H. "Young Adult Literature in the Classroom—Or Is It?" *English Journal* 86.3 (March 1997): 35-40.

Carlsen, G. Robert. *Books and the Teen-Age Reader*. New York: Bantam, 1971.

Chambers, Aidan. *The Reluctant Reader*. Oxford: Pergamon, 1969.

Chelton, Mary K. "Three in Five Public Library Users Are Youth: Implications of Survey Results from the National Center for Education Statistics." *Public Libraries* 36.2 (March/April 1997): 104-108.

Cope, Jim. "Beyond Voices of Readers: Students on School's Effects on Reading." *English Journal* 86.3 (March 1997): 18-23.

————. "Why I Teach, Promote, and Love Adolescent Literature: Confessions of a College English Professor." *Voices from the Middle* 5.2 (April 1998): 7-9.

Cullinan, Bernice E. *Read to Me: Raising Kids Who Love to Read*. New York: Scholastic, 1992.

Davidson, Judith, and David Koppenhaver. *Adolescent Literacy: What Works and Why*. 2nd ed. New York: Garland, 1993.

Decker, Barbara. "Aliteracy: What Teachers Can Do to Keep Johnny Reading." *Journal of Teacher Education* 37.6 (1986): 55-58.

Gentile, Lance, and Merna McMillan. "Why Won't Teenagers Read?" *Journal of Reading* 20.8 (1977): 649-654.

Humphrey, Jack W. "Do We Provide Children Enough Books to Read?" *The Reading Teacher* 44.2 (October 1990): 94.

Jones, Patrick. *Connecting Young Adults and Libraries: A How-To-Do-It Manual*. 2nd ed. New York: Neal-Schuman, 1998.

Lenox, Mary F. "The Reluctant Adolescent Reader: Action Steps for Librarians." *Catholic Library World* 55.8 (1984): 352-354.

Leonhardt, Mary. "Make Lemonade: How to Sweeten Your School's Climate for Reading." *School Library Journal* 44.1 (November 1998): 28-31.

————. *Parents Who Love to Read, Kids Who Don't: How It Happens and What You Can Do about It.* New York: Crown, 1995.

Mikulecky, Larry. *Aliteracy and a Changing View of Reading Goals.* ERIC, 1978. ERIC ED 157 052.

Myers, Walter Dean. "The Reluctant Reader." *Interracial Books for Children* 19.3/4 (1989): 14-15.

O'Rourke, W. "Are Parents an Influence on Adolescent Reading Habits?" *Journal of Reading* 22.4 (1979): 340-343.

Podl, Jody Brown. "Introducing Teens to the Pleasures of Reading." *Educational Leadership* 53.1 (September 1995): 56-57.

Reed, Arthea J. S. *Reaching Adolescents: The Young Adult Book and the School.* New York: Macmillan, 1994.

Rosenblatt, Louise. *The Reader, the Text, the Poem: The Transactional Theory of the Literary Work.* Carbondale, Il: Southern Illinois University Press, 1978.

Smith, Frank. *Understanding Reading: A Psycholinguistic Analysis of Reading and Learning to Read.* Hillsdale, NJ: Erlbaum, 1988.

Winkle, Alice W. "Research on Aliteracy: Why Johnny Doesn't Read." *Ohio Reading Teacher* 22.2 (1988): 40-47.

Chapter 2
Strategies for Reaching Reluctant Readers

Tying together research that has been done in the fields of language arts, library science, and reading education, this chapter will explore the various practical strategies educators and librarians can utilize to entice reluctant readers to read. Linda Clary identifies six specific strategies for getting young adults to read in her research: capitalize on interests, make reading material accessible, build a conducive environment, allow time to read in school, provide significant role models, and use motivational techniques (340). The strategies Clary identifies frame the discussions that follow.

Reading Role Models

Parents have a profound influence upon their child's reading habits. Children who are read to everyday, who are regularly taken to the public library, who are given books as gifts, are far less likely to grow up reluctant readers. Equally important is for children to see their own parents reading for enjoyment—that is, reading for themselves, in addition to reading to their children. The home that is filled with books, that subscribes to magazines and newspapers, and has parents or guardians who read them, is more likely to produce children who have an appreciation and enthusiasm for reading.

Unfortunately, many children grow up in homes void of these kinds of positive reading experiences. One can be hard pressed to find books of any kind in many homes. Parents who can read are otherwise aliterate, save for what needs to be read to function in the workplace. They do not subscribe to periodicals, do not buy books for themselves or their children, and do not read to their children. In many communities, a majority of families do not use their public library. One must also consider the fact that the adult literacy rate is still deplorable. Recent statistics for Tennessee, my home state, estimate 35-40 percent of adults are either completely or functionally illiterate. Tennessee has no monopoly on horrifying statistics like these, but consider that one in three adults in the state cannot read, and many of them are parents who should be serving as reading role models for their children. The damage caused by negative parental influence on a child's reading motivation cannot be underestimated. Without strong, positive influences in the earliest stages of a child's emergent literacy, he or she will be severely disadvantaged. Leslie Edmonds observes: "If young adults do not see value placed on reading at home or do not have peers that read, the value of reading may not be apparent" (375). Parents who could serve as reading role models for their preschool-age children, but choose not to, often proceed under the erroneous assumption that their children will receive enough of this influence in school.

What these parents fail to understand is that, by the time their child enters formal schooling, many crucial, foundational years of a child's emergent literacy development have already been lost. They enter school already at a disadvantage to other children who have parents actively influencing their child's literacy development. Parents should also not be so confident that this void in positive reading influences will be suddenly filled in school. Many teachers do read aloud to children regularly, if not on a daily basis, in the earliest grade levels, but this important ritual quickly dissipates in later years. By fourth grade, a teacher reading aloud to her class is an unusual occurrence, if it even happens at all. Teri Lesesne finds:

> The number of teachers reading aloud on a consistent basis to students decreases as the grade level increases, so that by middle school, a small percentage of teachers read aloud daily to their students. This is in spite of the finding that middle school students, especially middle school students who don't like to read or who can't read, report that they not only enjoy being read to, but they learn from it. (246)

Why does reading aloud become less a priority in the later grades? By the time children are in third grade, many already face the relentless onslaught of standardized testing they will endure the rest of their school years. The teacher is often forced into the position, by pressure from her principal or threat of termination if her class scores poorly, to divert all classroom activity to the cause of readying the students for successful test performance. Reading aloud books to children does not figure into this preparation.

Teachers are also faced with the dilemma of often working in a school which is run by principals who do not recognize the value of children being read aloud to or reading literature themselves. The act of reading, whether by the teacher or by the student, is not perceived as a "productive" activity, despite a mountain of evidence to the contrary. In an educational system that values only quantified results through standardized testing, the act of reading is not perceived as a productive activity. Thus, teachers have to abandon reading aloud for fear of being branded unproductive.

There is also the erroneous perception that reading education is only about children acquiring the necessary skills they need to decode and comprehend. It goes back to the simple-minded notion that children "learn to read and then read to learn." This attitude that reading is about skills and nothing more completely ignores the fact that if the impression is not made upon children that reading is an enjoyable, pleasurable experience, knowledge of those skills will be meaningless anyway. Once out of school, the children now grown into teenagers approaching adulthood will abandon reading altogether.

Reading aloud is one of the best means teachers have of impressing upon their students the notion that reading is more than about drills and worksheets. It is an opportunity to impress upon students the idea that the act of reading is something to be enjoyed, an idea that one hopes will instill in students a lifelong love for reading. This is an activity that cannot suddenly cease in third grade or any gràde. It is an activity that should persist through middle and high school. Gay Ivey stresses the important influence teachers reading aloud in the middle school classroom can have upon reluctant readers:

> Successful environments for struggling middle school readers involve interaction among students and interaction between students and teachers during literacy activities. One of these activities, alluded to previously, is the teacher read-aloud. There is no doubt that reading aloud to students is a powerful practice for promoting literacy appreciation and development, but I have found that read-alouds have specific benefits for struggling middle school readers. Introducing books and reading aloud to the class gives teachers a chance to show students that teachers themselves value the books they bring to the classroom, thus giving students the impression that reading is pleasurable and worthwhile. (375)

As Ivey says, the role the teacher plays as a reading role model in the classroom is crucial. Students need to see that their own teacher has a love for reading if she has any hope at all of instilling in them a similar enthusiasm. Reading aloud a favorite book is a particularly effective way for a teacher to share her personal enthusiasm.

Unfortunately, there are many teachers in classrooms today who have little interest in reading as the reluctant readers they teach. In their research into the reading practices of classroom teachers, Margaret

Mackey and Ingrid Johnston found that "a surprising number [of teachers] do not actually read for pleasure themselves" (29). I have found this to be too often the case in my work with teachers and students aspiring to be educators. I have been particularly distraught to find graduate students (pursuing a degree in reading education no less!) who are among the most resistant readers I have ever encountered. How disheartening it is to encounter students whose intention it is to be reading teachers to complain about having to read young adult fiction. How hard is it for a graduate student to read books written on a seventh or eighth grade reading level? It can be extremely difficult for them if they have never felt any enthusiasm or motivation for reading. Even more troubling is the fact that these students have little or no capacity for enjoying the books they read. How can they? For them, reading is a chore, a necessary evil to get them through school. They have no sense of what it is like to read for pleasure, to simply do it for the sake of doing it and enjoy the activity. How tragic that they have managed to come so far in life without experiencing the joy of reading, and how very troubling to contemplate that they will be "teaching reading" (whatever that means) in the classroom. I wish I could say that that is the exception rather than rule, but my own professional experience so far tells me it is not.

If young people do not have reading role models at home, they have to have them in the classroom, or they will surely be lost as readers. Children and adolescents are influenced by the adult authority figures in their lives. Parents and teachers are among the most influential, so they must accept the responsibility of being reading role models if there is any hope at all of turning kids into enthusiastic, lifelong readers.

Make Time for Reading

One of the most promising classroom instructional practices that can foster a student's enthusiasm for and involvement in reading is something most commonly known as Sustained Silent Reading (SSR). Two other popular names for the practice are "Drop Everything and Read" and "Free Voluntary Reading." Whatever the practice may be called, it is an example of genius in its simplicity. A block of time is set aside in the course of school day for students to simply read. How SSR is implemented in schools varies widely. Sometimes, the entire school simultaneously engages in the activity. It may be time set aside for students in their language arts or reading classes. The frequency and length of time given to the activity also varies. A school may engage in it at a daily, specified time. In a language arts class, the entire class time every other Friday may be devoted to SSR. One of the great things about SSR is that it is such a simple activity that there is plenty of flexibility in how it can be implemented.

Sustained silent reading can be a particularly effective means of getting reluctant readers to read because it sets aside a specific block of time for those students to focus on nothing else. Podl says of the benefits: "By giving my students classroom time, I can also be assured that every student will read something. Not everyone finishes every book, but I am convinced that more is being accomplished than would have had I passed out the books and given students two weeks to read them" (57). Adolescents have so many activities competing for their time—afterschool jobs, extracurricular activities, homework, sports, etc.—that they do not find the time to sit down and focus on reading. Timothy Rasinski observes:

> When students are unable or unwilling to set aside time for reading, then it is up to teachers and parents to build such time into daily school and home routines. Ten to thirty minutes per day should be sufficient time for students to discover that time spent reading can be a special and welcomed part of each day. (32)

Rasinski makes the excellent point that SSR impresses upon students that reading is special. By devoting a particular time of the day for students to focus on reading, schools are impressing upon them that reading is an important, worthwhile activity—a time to be anticipated and welcomed with enthusiasm.

Unfortunately, SSR is not as common a classroom practice as one would hope. Many principals do not see value in the activity. Worthy, Turner, and Moorman find that: "The most frequently cited reason for not providing regular opportunities for free choice reading was the pressure teachers felt to explicitly cover skills students needed to do well on the statewide competency test" (300). Good teachers recognize the value of SSR and want to implement the practice, but they are pressured by their superiors to engage only in activities that can produce more immediate, tangible outcomes. Worthy, Turner, and Moorman report:

> Many teachers said they would prefer to give students time to just read and not to answer questions. However, because of test pressure almost all teachers spent some instructional time preparing for the test, in fact, in some classrooms, teachers said that the test drove the curriculum, including skills lessons,

comprehension questions, response options, and reading logs. Despite the importance that almost every teacher placed on students' choice in reading materials, most said they felt pressure to restrict students' choices either explicitly or implicitly to some degree to "make the time count. (300)

Teachers who want to practice SSR, but have superiors who oppose it are in an awkward position. They have to use all of their powers of persuasion to convince them otherwise. There is plenty of research to support the claim that SSR does have a positive impact on students' reading ability, as well as collateral positive influence on writing and other communication skills. Faced with some solid research, principals opposed to SSR may relent in the face of such evidence. It is also always a good thing to let students speak for themselves. Collect student responses to SSR activities and share them with fellow faculty and the school administration to demonstrate its positive impact on student attitudes toward reading.

Give Readers More Choices

Self-selected reading perfectly complements sustained silent reading. During the designated reading time, students have the freedom to read whatever they like, whether it be something brought from home or something chosen from the school or classroom library. It does not necessarily have to be a book the student reads—it could be a comic book, magazine, or newspaper, depending on the flexibility of the teacher. The purpose of self-selected reading is to empower students— the freedom to choose something to read that interests them is motivating. Podl observes the intrinsic benefit there is in allowing students "to assert their independence by making choices about what they want to read" (57). Ivey agrees that self-selected reading can be a powerful motivational practice, particularly for reluctant readers, but cautions that common reading also has its benefits:

> The strong influence of self-selection on motivation to read makes a good case for free-choice reading, especially for struggling middle school readers. Still, for ease of dealing with comprehension instruction, promoting literary discussions, and developing content knowledge, teacher-selected, whole-class, common texts are sometimes necessary in middle school classrooms, so a balance between teacher-selected and student-selected reading must be maintained. (378)

One practice cannot be done at the expense of the other, of course, but self-selected reading is another powerful strategy to motivate students who resist reading. Empowering a student with choice is sometimes all that is needed to turn a non-reader on to reading.

Unfortunately, like sustained silent reading, self-selected reading is not as widely practiced as one would hope. There is, of course, the problem already discussed of there not being enough support or time for teachers to have an activity in which students can choose something to read and have the time in class to read it. There are additional barriers to self-selected reading.

The practice can only work if there is a wide variety of materials available from which students can choose. One might assume the school library would have more than enough varied materials from which to choose, but that is too often not the case. In their research, Worthy, Moorman, and Turner (1999) report that the types of reading materials students will find of most interest are not readily available in their school libraries or in classroom collections. Several causes of limited availability are cited: self-censorship on the part of librarians and teachers who object to materials they perceive to be graphic in sexual or violent content; lack of funding for "popular" materials; lack of durability and short "shelf life" of such materials; and the perception that popular reading materials are inappropriate for classroom and school library collections (21-22).

Another obstacle not cited is the lack of knowledge among teachers about adolescent literature. Many teacher education programs still do not require any course work in adolescent literature for students seeking a secondary teaching credential. Even the institutions that do require such course work do little more than pay lip service by requiring students one survey course in a body of literature that is nearly forty years old. A semester-long course is enough time to offer only the most superficial look at the enormously large and varied body of work written specifically for teenage audiences. Jeffrey Wilhelm suggests:

> Part of knowing how to teach good reading entails learning what techniques and what texts will work best with particular groups and particular individuals, and what books will be new, surprising, and challenging—helping the student to grow. This requires getting to know students, their current interests and abilities, and their own stories of what and how they read. (34)

That one required course is not enough to give classroom teachers the knowledge they need to encourage and offer their students a variety of choices. There is also the issue that Walter Dean Myers raises of students needing stories that are culturally relevant to them:

> What I am suggesting is that we do not restrict materials available to the reluctant reader but rather pay special attention to such material as might facilitate reading. That is, a stronger emphasis on material that is culturally familiar or which considers more specifically the social milieu of the reader. (15)

A teacher with a racially or ethnically diverse class, or one that is predominantly black or Latino, whose students are reluctant readers, is going to have to consider what kinds of books can be offered to these students that will speak to their experiences, to what they know and believe. Myers goes on to say: "But the idea that Black books might facilitate reading by some Black readers, or that books with Spanish or Asian background might be more be more suitable for Spanish or Asian children who are also reluctant readers, seems to have struck a sore point" (15). There is still resistance to this type of "multiculturalist" approach. When good, thoughtful practices are trivialized into "isms," it is easy for them to become polarized. The reality is that kids who do not like to read, regardless of their race or ethnic origin, will respond most positively to reading stories that speak to their experiences. They want characters and situations with which they can identify. A black teenager growing up in south central Los Angeles where gang violence is a constant is a lot more likely to connect with a story like Myers's *Scorpions* than they are with Paul Zindel's *The Pigman*. Teachers need to consider this if they are going to give readers choices. They need to make available to their students choices that make sense. As Linda Moniuszko observes: "When given the opportunity to read about relevant subjects that they value, students will choose to read" (34).

Make Reading a Purposeful Experience

Relevancy is a very important issue for reluctant teen readers. The perception that reading is drudgery, an assigned activity without any purpose other than to complete a teacher's assignment and earn a decent grade, is a major factor in why so many adolescents resist reading. Mackey and Johnston observe:

> If your main experience with reading involves texts chosen by someone else, with constant checks on your progress and comprehension; if your usual strategies are laborious rather

than free-flowing; if your main experience for reading for pleasure is based on nonfiction with a high value placed on a tangible return for your effort; if any or all of these experiences apply to you then why would it cross your mind to associate reading with pleasure? (27)

Most teenagers manage to get through school with having few, if any, experiences with reading that they can call pleasurable. That is why they go on to be aliterate adults. It is not as if these students could not derive pleasure from reading if given the opportunity. Timothy Rasinski observes: "Making connections between students' specific interests and books that match those interests can also spark the internal motivation that will carry a reader through a book" (32). If teachers and the curriculum they use made an effort to capitalize on their students' own potential reading interests, there would be a lot more students graduating from high school remembering positive reading experiences and having an enthusiasm to read the rest of their lives.

Nothing turns an adolescent off to reading faster than hearing a librarian or teacher tell them that they should read because "it's for their own good." I don't care how good a rapport you have with your students, it will never be enough to convince them that they should read the book you want them to read just because it's good for them. You may be right. You probably are, but even the most motivated readers won't buy that. What you see as relevant is a far cry from what your students' see. How many times have you heard frustrated students in your classroom ask with a heavy sigh "Why do we have to know this?" or blurt out "This is stupid! Why do we have to waste our time reading this?" I heard that every day when I taught high school. Did that make me a bad teacher? I know there's a lot more I could have done to motivate my students, but even the most innovative, creative, motivational teacher inevitably hears those comments and questions from students. Ivey finds that:

> Although reading and writing were scarcely mentioned as favorites, students did not complain about reading and writing when they were used to accomplish some meaningful task. It is not surprising that middle school readers need real purposes for reading, given that motivation is highest when students engage in tasks for their own intrinsic reasons. For middle school students who struggle with reading, having authentic purpose is especially crucial. (377)

This "authentic purpose" for reading that Ivey speaks of is what students need to perceive if they are to be motivated about reading. Students will get a sense of this purpose if teachers empower them to have choices about the kinds of materials they read. They will have a sense of purpose if a teacher gives her students an opportunity to engage with what they read. I'm not talking about Accelerated Reader® tests, book reports, or quizzes. I'm talking about some real, honest to goodness engagement—opportunities for students to reflect, discuss, debate, speculate, and critique what they read with their teacher and amongst themselves. I'm talking about engaging readers 'higher order thinking" activities that our young (and older) people are so sorely lacking in—the kinds of activities that are sacrificed to a mindless, sterile environment of "readability ratings" and standardized testing. Students will be more likely to read if we make the purpose of reading more than just what you have to do to fill in the blanks at the end.

Another way to make reading more appealing and relevant to students is to connect it to other activities and to real life. It is important to impress upon students that reading does not have to be an isolated activity. Books do not have to exist in a vacuum. Why not show students films that have been inspired by the book they read in class? Why not adapt a script and act out a scene from a story? Rasinski recommends many excellent activities that can follow reading to make the experience more relevant to students.

> Experiences students have in school should be related to books on similar topics. The experiences can take a variety of forms. Field trips, special speakers and guests in the school, movies and videotapes, role plays, skits, experiments, artifact collections, demonstrations and the like can swell interest to the point where further reading on the subject is a desired and natural extension of the activity. Watching a motion picture or video portrayal of a book can stimulate reading in two ways. First, the visual portrayal creates an interest in the topic of the book itself. Second, the movie or video creates and/or activates the required background information in readers to insure that they will comprehend the book. (31)

I found what Rasinski says about showing video versions in conjunction with texts to be true in my own classroom teaching experience. Students were left with a much better understanding of a Shakespearean play after they saw it acted out. It was, in fact, so successful, I concluded that it might be just as well to have them watch the play *instead* of reading it. After all, a play is written for performance. Of course, readers will get more out of a play watching it being performed rather than reading it.

Whatever course you choose to make reading more pleasurable and purposeful for students, the key to any successful activity is to keep the students at the center. You have to know something of your students, particularly their interests. You have to be willing to be flexible about how you meet their interests. If you find the curriculum working against you, you have to decide if you are teaching for the curriculum or for your students. If you really do want to turn your students into enthusiastic, lifelong lovers of reading, you have to be willing to take some risks on their behalf.

Promote Reading through Special Activities

Reluctant readers can often be motivated through special programs offered by a public or school library, or in the classroom. The programs do not necessarily have to be expensive, or require a great deal of materials or time to implement. There is enough to choose from to satisfy any educator's level of ability or ambition. What all of these programs do have in common, however, is an attempt to engage students with the books they read—by giving them the freedom to choose what they read and to meaningfully interact with the stories they read.

In North Carolina, for example, a program called "Battle of the Books" has been staged in middle schools to encourage readers. Students choose from a list of young adult books compiled by school librarians and engage in a competition that is not geared toward accruing the most points or scoring the highest percentage, but rather for the purpose of learning that reading is exciting and fun (Mallison, 1991). Mary Krogness developed a "reading race" in an attempt to motivate her reluctant adolescent readers. In this month-long contest, Krogness offered points to students for literally anything they read, including directions, obituaries, and recipes. The spirit of competition, Krogness found, encouraged her students who previously would resist reading anything to read fiction, nonfiction, and even poetry in an attempt to accumulate the most points. Krogness kept the activity fun by making the act of reading itself the focus. She points out that: "I purposely didn't require my readers to write or make oral book reports, answer questions about their reading, or indulge in any other kind of foolproof evaluation scheme" (77). Krogness believed that asking students to follow up their reading with outcome devices like that would only discourage them. Her sole purpose in the activity was to motivate her students to read and it was highly successful. Now some people will argue (I among them) that reducing the act of reading to a matter of earning points is not desirable, but Krogness sees the competition as the means rather than the end. Competition will lead some reluctant readers to reading, but the goal is that, once the competition is over, students will continue to read without that incentive. Note the similarity of Krogness's homemade program to the pre-packaged Accelerated Reader® and Reading Counts® programs that so many schools squander thousands of dollars upon.

One of the most exciting ways to motivate young people to read is to bring authors and readers together. Telling kids that they will have the opportunity to meet the author of the book they are reading is one of the best ways I know to get them excited. Young people do not understand or appreciate how much work goes into creating a book, and the insight they gain into that process from interaction with an author opens up for them a whole new exciting perspective on reading. They also have the chance to have conversations about what they read with the creator of it, a unique, richly rewarding opportunity. Author and publisher Lyn Miller-Lachmann has this to say about author visits:

> I cannot emphasize enough the value of author visits to a group of problem readers. Every time I speak to such a group, at least one of the students tells me this is the first time he or she has met a "real author." With students whose major experience in school is one of failure, the arrival of an author who is willing to give his or her time and to listen is an important, memorable event. (10)

The location of your library or school and your funding situation will determine whom you can invite and how frequently you can host such programs, but many communities have local authors within driving distance. The best way to arrange an author visit is to contact a marketing representative of a publishing company. Most publishers have someone whose responsibility it is to arrange author appearances. They are always very knowledgeable and helpful people who can give you the information you need to host such a program.

A simple, cost-free, but often overlooked way of promoting reading is to simply market books to kids. I never cease to be amazed at how few schools have librarians and teachers working closely together. How often do teachers bring their classes to the school library for the purpose of just browsing the shelves and checking out books? How often does the school librarian have an opportunity to booktalk a variety of titles to a class? Those two activities are probably among the simplest and most effective in encouraging kids to read.

Works Cited

Carter, Betty. "Formula for Failure: Reading Levels and Readability Formulas Do Not Create Lifelong Readers." *School Library Journal* 46.7 (July 2000): 34-37.

Clary, Linda Mixon. "Getting Adolescents to Read." *Journal of Reading* 34.5 (February 1991): 340-345.

Edmonds, Leslie. "Selling Reading: Library Service to Reluctant Adolescent Readers." *Illinois Libraries* (June 1986): 374-377.

Ivey, Gay. "Reflections on Teaching Struggling Middle School Readers." *Journal of Adolescent and Adult Literacy* 42.5 (February 1999): 372-381.

Krogness, Mary Mercer. *Just Teach Me, Mrs. K: Talking, Reading, and Writing with Resistant Adolescent Learners*. Portsmouth, NH: Heinemann, 1995.

Lesene, Teri S. "Reading Aloud to Build Success in Reading." *Into Focus: Understanding and Creating Middle School Readers*. Eds. Kylene Beers and Barbara G. Samuels. Norwood, MA: Christopher-Gordon, 1998: 245-260.

Mackey, Margaret, and Ingrid Johnston. "The Book Resisters: Ways of Approaching Reluctant Teenage Readers." *School Libraries Worldwide* 2.1 (1996) 25-38.

Mallison, Francis. "Battle of the Books: Middle School Reading Motivation." *North Carolina Libraries* (Summer 1991): 93-94.

Miller-Lachmann, Lyn. "Publishing and Writing for the Reluctant Reader." *Hi/Low Handbook: Encouraging Literacy in the 1990s*. New York: Bowker, 1990.

Moniuszko, Linda K. "Motivation: Reaching Reluctant Readers Ages 14-17." *Journal of Reading* 36.1 (September 1992): 32-34.

Myers, Walter Dean. "The Reluctant Reader." *Interracial Books for Children* 19.3/4 (1989): 14-15.

Podl, Jody Brown. "Introducing Teens to the Pleasures of Reading." *Educational Leadership* 53.1 (September 1995): 56-57.

Wilhelm, Jeffrey D. *You Gotta Be the Book: Teaching Engaged and Reflective Reading with Adolescents.* New York: Teachers College Press, 1997.

Winograd, Peter, and Scott G. Paris. "A Cognitive and Motivational Agenda for Reading Instruction." *Educational Leadership* 46 (December 1988/January 1989): 30-36.

Worthy, Jo. "Removing Barriers to Voluntary Reading for Reluctant Readers: The Role of School and Classroom Libraries." *Language Arts* 73.7 (November 1996): 483-492.

Worthy, Jo, Margo Turner, and Megan Moorman. "The Precarious Place of Self-Selected Reading." *Language Arts* 75.4 (April 1998): 296-303.

———. "What Johnny Likes to Read Is Hard to Find in School." *Reading Research Quarterly* 34.1 (January/February/March 1999): 12-27.

Chapter 3
Resources for Reluctant Readers: Fiction

High/Low vs. Traditional Fiction

True high/low books differ distinctly from traditional fiction in both content and physical dimensions. Paperback high/low books are smaller and thinner than the typical young adult trade paperback. The use of wide margins, extensive white space, and larger than usual font size are typical features of these books. The typical high/low story is almost entirely plot-driven and the style dictated by controlled vocabulary. Helen Williams notes that:

> High interest/low-readability level books were developed because of a perceived need for reading material which would assure some measure of reading success for deficient and reluctant readers. . . . Design and format were manipulated to minimize stigmatization or the likely humiliation of adolescents being seen carrying a "kiddie book." (33)

High/low books were developed for the reasons Williams cites, but they do not address the needs of aliterate adolescents who are not reading not because of a disability or unfamiliarity with English, but because they have not been introduced to books that would be of interest to them.

High/low books are excellent for students with poor developmental skills, whether due to learning disabilities or gaps in their education, who are seeking to improve their reading level. They are good for non-native speakers of English who desire to improve their reading proficiency in English. These books will not, however, entice kids who are able to read but choose not to. If fiction is the type of book that appeals to a reluctant reader, the books that will interest them are series fiction, short stories, or the traditional young adult novel.

Series Books

There are many librarians, parents, and teachers who look down upon mass market paperback series books, dismissing them outright as formulaic, predictable, and superficial. It is presumed that because books are part of a series, they are necessarily badly constructed and poorly written. The reality is that a great deal of skill and talent is needed to create a series that will appeal to teen readers, and it is even more challenging to continue coming up with new stories that will keep kids interested. Series books have always been popular with young readers. I grew up reading *Doc Savage* and *The Hardy Boys*, who were around long before I was born and are still popular. The same is true of *Nancy Drew*. The kids from *Sweet Valley* may have graduated from high school to college, but it's still a very popular, widely read franchise among young adolescent girls.

Aesthetically speaking, series books usually are not as "good" as a "good" mainstream young adult novel. They do have the weaknesses for which many adults disparage them: predictability and superficiality. But what adults consider weaknesses are what many adolescent readers view as strengths. Barbara Samuels argues that "formula novels and series books fulfill an important role in the reading development of young teens" (351). Young teens read series books precisely because they are predictable. Teens want to read the same story over and over again because it gives them great comfort to know what they can expect. Series books help children and younger adolescents who might otherwise dislike reading become comfortable with it.

Silk Makowski makes the reasonable argument that series fiction should not be judged by the standards applied to other novels. She makes this contrast between the two:

> Monographs give you *everything* in one grand experience. Monographs are a one-night stand. Series, on the other hand, are *built for the long haul*. Everything about them, plot, characters, setting, style of writing, even the physical *look* of the book, contributes to that aim, which is to provide you, the reader, with the same grand experience night after night, week after week, year after year, *ad infinitum*. (349-350)

Makowski argues that once series fiction is recognized as a genre unto itself and is evaluated by criteria relevant to it, it will be better appreciated and understood.

When adolescents want to read series books, their interest should be welcomed, not discouraged. Librarians and teachers who have reluctant readers on their hands should go out of their way to encourage them to read a series. It may be just the thing those kids need to finally make a meaningful connection with books. Advocating for acceptance of series books in the classroom, English teachers Louann Reid and Ruth Cline argue: "Making room for series books will help students make room for other reading. Interests and abilities constantly develop, and many readers move on from their obsession with series books to obsessions with other titles" (72). There is plenty to choose from in series books now for both genders and every imaginable area of interest. Adventure, mystery, romance, and horror have always been among the most popular genres for series fiction, but there are also series built around such subjects as hospital emergency rooms, Internet technology, science fiction, search and rescue, and sports (extreme and otherwise). There are good series now available for teens looking for Christian fiction. If you think television is your adversary, make it your ally by stocking your shelves with books based on the programs teens watch, like *Buffy the Vampire Slayer* and *Dawson's Creek*. Popularity is fleeting, particularly when it comes to teens. Five years ago, you could not buy enough *Animorphs* and *Fear Street*. Now you can't give those books away. Go to the section in your local chain bookstore designated "young adult" and you are likely to find nothing but series books. It's a good way to keep up to date on the latest series being published.

The young teen who eventually tires of reading R. L. Stine, *Sweet Valley*, or whatever is their series of choice will eventually move on to more challenging literature. Catherine Ross argues "series books do *not* enfeeble readers or render them unfit for anything else" (233). I have seen it too many times to count in my work as a public librarian. Series books can be an important key to enticing kids into a lifetime of reading.

Short Stories

Donald R. Gallo, editor of many excellent short story anthologies for young adults, states what should be obvious to us all: "For reluctant readers as well as for less able students, short stories can be the most accessible and satisfying literary form—primarily because they are short" (333). Yet, short story collections are among those books in the young adult collection that collect the most dust. The few times I have encountered a teen requesting short stories, it's been for an assignment. Edgar Allan Poe collections are the only short stories I have ever known a young adult to ask for to read for his or her enjoyment. What's the deal with short stories? Why do librarians and teachers give them short shrift?

Look at any middle or high school English textbook, and you will find dozens of short stories clustered around various themes. The better textbooks might feature a story by a real young adult author like M. E. Kerr, Norma Fox Mazer, or Walter Dean Myers. The rest will be the same old stuff we probably read when we were students: stories by such authors as Nathaniel Hawthorne, Ernest Hemingway, F. Scott Fitzgerald, John Updike, and Edith Wharton. Now I am not suggesting there is anything wrong with reading these authors—if you are an adult—but let's face it, few teenagers will find these authors relevant to their own lives. Reluctant readers, especially, will not be motivated to read such authors. Gallo recommends "teachers who want stories that are more likely to attract middle school readers in the first place, regardless of content, will be more successful if the main character or characters in the stories are teenagers at the same age as, or slightly older than, the students in their class" (334). Even if you are working with a better textbook that actually includes young adult authors, teens may still be reluctant to read these stories because the textbook itself carries a stigma. Gallo observes: "Part of the lack of appeal is no doubt the typical textbook format, making books like this look as if they are more for work than enjoyment" (336). The reader is left with the impression that all short stories are probably boring, and are forever unpleasantly associated with schoolwork.

Librarians also share complicity in turning teens off to short stories. Think of where we put short story anthologies: the 800s in nonfiction! How many non-librarians know, or would ever guess, that short fiction (emphasize the word "fiction") would be found in nonfiction. I have lost count of how many confused kids I have tried to convince that the short stories in the nonfiction section are fiction. They have a hard time grasping that incongruity, and I don't blame them. It does not make much sense. Maybe if young adults knew where to look for short stories, they might be more inclined to read them. Serendipity plays a far more significant role when readers are selecting fiction. With the short stories stuck in nonfiction, nobody is going to find them unless they want to. The odd thing is that not all short story collections are in nonfiction. The compiled or edited anthologies end up with a Dewey number in the nonfiction section. Collections of stories by a single author, however, whether they are interconnected or not, are likely to end up in fiction, yet another incongruity to further confuse our readers.

There is plenty for librarians and teachers to like about short stories. For librarians, there is the attraction of being able to tell one story in its entirety as a booktalk. Depending on their length and complexity, a short story can be a great read aloud for middle or even high school age students. Gallo explains what a valuable teaching tool the short story can be: "For one thing, the length of short stories allows the story to be introduced, read, and discussed during one class period. Brevity means teachers can let students spend time focusing on response" (337). Short stories can enable teachers to expose students to a wide variety of authors and themes that would not be possible with novels. They are more "teachable" than novels, too. It is easier to map out the plot, and the analysis and discussion of the story's dimensions is obviously less involved.

One would think there is much about short stories that would appeal to young adult readers. The most obvious is that they are short. Gallo notes: "An average short story takes less than one-tenth of the time to read than a typical novel does" (333). What better way to appease the impatience and short attention span of a reluctant reader than with short stories? The shorter the better. How many times when recommending titles have you heard the inevitable question: "How many pages are there?" Brevity should be a huge selling point, but it's not always. The stigma of short stories being associated with schoolwork can be profound for some teens. Reluctant readers should be encouraged to "read around" in an anthology, impressing upon them that there is no obligation to read the whole book cover to cover. I'm not certain how we come to instill the absurd notion in people that if one begins a book, one must finish it, but it is that sense of obligation that helps turn young adults off to short story collections.

It is unfortunate that short story anthologies are so unpopular with young adults because there are so many wonderful collections being published specifically for them. What can we do to lure more young adults to short stories? We can start by giving them more visibility. Booktalking and displaying them more prominently is a good place to start.

If young adults are turned off to the genre because of the textbook stigma, we can recommend collections by a single author they may find appealing. Richard Peck, a longtime young adult favorite, published the Newbery Award-winning *A Long Way to Chicago* (Dial, 1998) and *A Year Down Yonder* (Dial, 2000), collections of interconnected, humorous short stories featuring a memorable Grandma. Readers who savor Francesca Lia Block's flowery, psychedelic prose in the *Weetzie Bat* novels will enjoy *Girl Goddess #9* (HarperCollins/Joanna Cotler, 1996). For young adults who enjoy the fantastic, and they are legion, they can lose themselves in Jane Yolen's *Twelve Impossible Things Before Breakfast* (Harcourt Brace, 1997). Readers who appreciate touches of humor with their supernatural tales will enjoy Vivian Van de Velde's *Curses, Inc.* (Harcourt Brace/Jane Yolen, 1997). Older teens who became devoted Rob Thomas fans with *Rats Saw God* will surely take to *Doing Time: Notes from the Undergrad* (Simon & Schuster, 1997), a collection of related stories that uncannily reflect the attitudes and voices of contemporary young adults. Younger teens may find inspiration in Michael J. Rosen's *The Heart Is Big Enough* (Harcourt Brace, 1997), a collection of stories featuring young adolescents overcoming adversities of various kinds.

Anthologies may be a harder sell. Readers will find a range of voices and styles. Some stories will appeal and some will not. What sells an anthology to readers is a good theme. In recent years, compilers, editors, and publishers have been very creative in coming up with themes and a "packaging" approach to short story anthologies that do have potentially broad young adult appeal. Lois Duncan produced *Night Terrors: Stories of Shadows and Substance* (Simon & Schuster, 1996), an anthology of mystery and suspense stories by young adult favorites like Annette Curtis Klause, Chris Lynch, and Joan Lowry Nixon. What young adult does not enjoy mystery and suspense? Sporting a spooky, mysterious cover, and featuring authors readers know and like, it's hard for a collection like this to miss. Duncan edited another appealing collection recently called *Trapped: Cages of Mind and Body* (Simon & Schuster, 1998). Once again, the appeal of the theme is almost guaranteed. What adolescent does not feel trapped in some way? Here, too, Duncan taps outstanding, popular young adult authors like Francesca Lia Block and Rob Thomas. Harry Mazer's *Twelve Shots: Outstanding Short Stories about Guns* (Delacorte, 1997) has a cover featuring images of a revolver, bullets, military medals, and a chalk outline of a body that is sure to get attention. The authors Mazer assembles (Ron Koertge, Walter Dean Myers, Richard Peck, and Rita Williams-Garcia among them) truly are outstanding, and they all contribute exceptional pieces. Marion Dane Bauer's *Am I Blue?: Coming Out of the Silence* (HarperCollins, 1994) addresses gay and lesbian themes with stories by such distinguished authors as Nancy Garden, Lois Lowry, William Sleator, and Jacqueline Woodson. Teenagers working is a theme of two anthologies that appeared in the same year. Anne Mazer's *Working Days: Short Stories about Teenagers at Work* (Persea, 1997) and Anita Silvey's *Help Wanted: Short Stories about Young People Working* (Little, Brown, 1997) do not have the stellar author lineups of other collections or the most appealing covers, but they do appeal to a subject all young adults are interested in. After getting a driver's license, having a part-time job is one of the most important rites of passage in a teenager's life. The stories in both collections feature teens working at jobs, many of them their first, for a variety of reasons: to help contribute to family expenses; to cover their own expenses; or to fulfill some dream like buying a car.

No one is better skilled at compiling anthologies with strong teen appeal than Donald Gallo. He consistently produces exceptional short story anthologies for young adults, beginning with *Sixteen: Short Stories by Outstanding Writers for Young Adults* (Delacorte, 1984) to his most recent, *On the Fringe* (Dial, 2001). In *No Easy Answers: Short Stories about Teenagers Making Tough Choices* (Delacorte, 1997), YA favorites like M. E. Kerr and David Klass contribute provocative stories featuring teens facing tough ethical and moral dilemmas. If you want to see an example of an exceptional short story collection for young adults, look at any one compiled and edited by Gallo.

Publishers are already doing their part producing excellent collections. It is time for librarians and teachers to do our part. Instead of using the stale stories in textbooks that students hate, teachers can use those that have been written specifically for young adults. Public and school librarians need to pull our short story anthologies from obscurity in the nonfiction shelves and start marketing them to readers through booktalks and displays.

Young Adult Novels

Reluctant teenage readers will not read high/low novels, and they will not read classics traditionally taught in the English curriculum. From series fiction, reluctant readers can "graduate" to young adult novels, or they might not even need the transition, finding a particular author or book that grabs them immediately. Young adult novels are books every adolescent, reluctant reader or not, should read because, as Gallo (1992) observes, "young adult novels are valuable tools for helping teenagers to understand themselves and to see their place in a world that is far different from the one in which many of us English teachers grew up" (26). Samuels (1992) notes that young adult novels address the developmental concerns and psychological needs of adolescents (29). Young adult novels also serve as an important transition for all teens, particularly reluctant readers, between children's literature, adult books, and the classics.

Young adult literature came into its own in the late 1960s with the publication of landmark titles like S. E. Hinton's *The Outsiders*, Robert Cormier's *The Chocolate War*, and Paul Zindel's *The Pigman*. Those and other pioneering authors like M. E. Kerr, Harry Mazer, Norma Fox Mazer, Walter Dean Myers, and Richard Peck helped define young adult literature as a body of literature of great quality worthy of serious study. Over thirty years later, there is a vast canon of distinguished fiction and nonfiction for young adults. Unfortunately, young adult literature is still greatly marginalized in the publishing industry. Mainstream literary critics do not give it serious consideration. It gets only token attention from venues like *The New York Times Book Review*. There have been some notable advances in giving young adult literature the attention it deserves. The National Book Awards recently revived its young people's category and distinguished young adult novels have been recognized. The *Los Angeles Times* Book Prizes now includes a young adult fiction category. The American Library Association's Best Books for Young Adults and the new Michael L. Printz Award for Excellence in Young Adult Literature also help in distinguishing the best that is being published for young adults.

The best of young adult fiction is written with teens specifically in mind, featuring characters, conflicts, and themes to which they can relate. Read a novel by authors like Joan Bauer, Michael Cadnum, Robert Cormier, Sarah Dessen, Chris Lynch, Han Nolan, or Jacqueline Woodson, and it will be obvious how aesthetically sophisticated, emotionally rewarding, and intellectually challenging young adult literature at its best can be. Young adult novels can be as deep and provocative as any of the so-called classics, but they go one better because they speak directly to teens about people and subjects which matter most to them.

Like adult fiction, young adult novels span all genres. Will Hobbs is a master of adventure stories featuring complex, strong male protagonists. Nancy Werlin crafts rich, compelling suspense stories. Rob Thomas has an uncanny ability to tap into teen sensibilities in his coming-of-age stories. The canon of young adult literature is old enough and large enough to offer great novels in every area of interest.

Not all young adult novels will appeal to reluctant readers. Stories that are particularly funny, scary, or suspenseful will probably have the strongest appeal. The book should be relatively short, less than two hundred pages, and have an attractive cover. Teens pay a great deal of attention to cover art when they are considering whether or not to read it. The chapters should be brief, the plot fast-paced and relatively simple, and the style lean and straightforward. Having a wide variety of young adult novels spanning all genres in your classrooms and library is the best chance you have of enticing the reluctant reader to pick up a book.

Works Cited

Gallo, Donald R. "Listening to Readers: Attitudes Toward the Young Adult Novel." *Reading Their World: The Young Adult Novel in the Classroom*. Portsmouth, NH: Boynton Cook/Heinemann, 1992.

———. "Short Stories—Long Overdue." *Into Focus: Understanding and Creating Middle School Readers*. Eds. Kylene Beers and Barbara G. Samuels. Norwood, MA: Christopher-Gordon, 1998.

Makowski, Silk. "Serious about Series: Selection Criteria for a Neglected Genre." *Voice of Youth Advocates* 16.6 (February 1994): 349-351.

Reid, Louann, and Ruth K. J. Cline. "Our Repressed Reading Addictions: Teachers and Young Adult Series Books." *English Journal* 86.3 (March 1997): 68-70.

Ross, Catherine Sheldrick. "If They Read Nancy Drew, So What? Series Book Readers Talk Back." *Library and Information Science Review* 17 (1995): 201-236.

Samuels, Barbara G. "Creating Lifetime Readers: A Novel Idea." *Into Focus: Understanding and Creating Middle School Readers*. Eds. Kylene Beers and Barbara G. Samuels. Norwood, MA: Christopher-Gordon, 1998.

———. "The Young Adult Novel as Transitional Literature." *Reading Their World: The Young Adult Novel in the Classroom*. Portsmouth, NH: Boynton Cook/Heinemann, 1992.

Sullivan, Edward. "Solving the Short Story Puzzle." *School Library Journal* (January 1999): 38-39.

Williams, Helen E. "Characterizations in High-Interest/Low-Vocabulary Level Fiction." *School Library Journal* (February 1987): 31-33.

Guides to Fiction with Reluctant Reader Appeal

Bodart, Joni Richards. *The World's Best Thin Books: What to Read When Your Book Report Is Due Tomorrow.* Lanham, MD: Scarecrow, 2000.
Over ninety young adult titles divided into three categories of thinnest, thinner, and thin, none over two hundred pages, are cited in this extremely helpful guide. Bodart offers full bibliographic information for each title, outlines the characters and major themes, and suggests booktalk ideas. Every school library and public library reader's advisory desk should be equipped with a copy.

Fast and Easy. The New York Public Library, Office of Young Adult Services. 2000.
Updated every few years, this annotated list of fiction and nonfiction, selected by young adult librarians, identifies books that have potential appeal for reluctant readers ages twelve to eighteen.

Quick Picks for Reluctant Young Adult Readers. American Library Association, Young Adult Library Services Association.
An annual list of fiction and nonfiction chosen by a committee of YALSA members recommending recently published books with particular appeal for reluctant teen readers.

Sherman, Gale W., and Bette D. Ammon. *Rip-Roaring Reads for Reluctant Teen Readers.* Englewood, CO: Libraries Unlimited, 1993.
Forty fiction and nonfiction recommendations are evenly distributed between middle and high school grades. The authors include plot summaries, booktalk ideas, suggestions for classroom activities, and biographical information about the author(s) for each entry.

Twenty-Five Essential Short Story Anthologies

Bauer, Marion Dane, ed. *Am I Blue? Coming Out from the Silence.* New York: HarperCollins: 1994.

Blume, Judy, ed. *Places I Never Meant to Be: Original Stories by Censored Writers.* New York: Simon & Schuster, 1999.

Cart, Michael, ed. *Tomorrowland: Stories about the Future.* New York: Scholastic, 1999.

————. *Love and Sex: Ten Stories of Truth.* Simon & Schuster, 2001.

Duncan, Lois, ed. *Night Terrors: Stories of Shadow and Substance.* New York: Simon & Schuster, 1996.

————. *On the Edge: Stories at the Brink.* New York: Simon & Schuster, 2000.

————. *Trapped! Cages of Mind and Body.* New York: Simon & Schuster, 1998.

Gallo, Donald R., ed. *Connections: Short Stories by Outstanding Writers for Young Adults.* New York: Doubleday, 1989.

————. *Join In: Multiethnic Short Stories for by Outstanding Writers for Young Adults.* Delacorte, 1993.

————. *No Easy Answers: Short Stories about Teenagers Making Tough Choices.* New York: Delacorte, 1997.

————. *On the Fringe.* New York: Dial, 2001.

————. *Short Circuits: Thirteen Shocking Stories by Outstanding Writers for Young Adults.* New York:Delacorte, 1992.

————. *Sixteen: Short Stories for by Outstanding Writers for Young Adults.* New York: Delacorte, 1984.

————. *Time Capsule: Short Stories about Teenagers through the Twentieth Century.* New York: Delacorte, 1999.

————. *Ultimate Sports: Short Stories for by Outstanding Writers for Young Adults.* New York: Delacorte, 1995.

Lyons, Mary E., ed. *Raw Head and Bloody Bones: African-American Tales of the Supernatural.* New York: Scribner's, 1991.

Mazer, Anne, ed. *America Street: A Multicultural Anthology of Stories.* New York: Persea, 1993.

————. *Working Days: Short Stories about Teenagers at Work.* New York: Persea, 1997.

Mazer, Harry, ed. *Twelve Shots: Outstanding Short Stories about Guns.* New York: Delacorte, 1997.

Muse, Daphne, ed. *Prejudice: Stories about Hate, Ignorance, Revelation, and Transformation.* New York: Hyperion, 1995.

Rochman, Hazel, and Darlene Z. McCampbell, eds. *Leaving Home.* New York: HarperCollins, 1997.

Singer, Marilyn, ed. *I Believe in Water: Twelve Brushes with Religion.* HarperCollins, 2000.

Thomas, Joyce Carol, ed. *A Gathering of Flowers: Stories about Being Young in America.* New York: HarperCollins, 1993.

Weiss, M. Jerry, and Helen S. Weiss, eds. *From One Experience to Another.* New York: Forge, 1997.

Yep, Laurence, ed. *American Dragons: Twenty-Five Asian American Voices.* New York: HarperCollins, 1993.

Chapter 4
Resources for Reluctant Readers:
Comics and Graphic Novels

A Misunderstood Medium

Graphic novels are often a misunderstood medium among many librarians and teachers and, consequently, are dismissed without any serious consideration. Their unique substance and style should have a place in both the classroom and the library. Although they are not comic books, graphic novels are a close relative, and that may be a significant contributing factor to why negative perceptions persist about them. Richard Gagnier observes that "it's not unusual for YA [young adult] librarians to disdain graphic novels. Neither has it been unusual in my experience for them to be judged by harsher standards than other types of literature" (143). There is a presumption by those who would dismiss these books that, because the story is more visual than textual, it is less substantive. When it comes to middle and high school age young adults, for whom these books have the most appeal, many adults believe that any book employing illustrations is too young, too juvenile for that audience. Books with pictures are "kid stuff," something an adolescent should be beyond reading. This is the same argument librarians and teachers use against making picture books available to adolescents.

What Are Graphic Novels?

If graphic novels are not comic books, what are they? Keith DeCandido defines graphic novels as "a self-contained story that uses a combination of text and art to articulate plot. It is equivalent in content to a long short story or short novel and in some ways a larger version of a comic book" (50). Aviva Rothschild champions the aesthetic merits of the genre:

Graphic novels use words and pictures in ways that transcend ordinary art and text, and their creators are more than writers and artists. The artist must have a director's eye for shadow, angle, setting, and costume. The writer has to know when the text speaks and when the art speaks, avoiding redundancy. In the ideal graphic novel, the text does not distract from the art or vice versa; the eye flows naturally from element to element, creating a whole that a text-only book cannot match. (xiv)

Graphic novels can be a single story or a set of interrelated stories that are told in a sequential art form. As DeCandido points out, graphic novels are not "overgrown comics," but rather more akin to a long short story or novella. It is true that superhero stories are among the most popular of graphic novel titles, but they are by no means limited to those themes. As Katharine Kan, a graphic novel expert explains:

> Lots of the trade comics popular among male teens come from the major comics publishers Marvel and DC; they feature costumed super heroes such as Superman, Batman, Spiderman, the X-men, etc. While YA [young adult] collections should get these in order to attract more male readers into the libraries, these comics are not the only trade comics available. Most of the truly creative work is published by independent publishers; these books are usually in black-and-white and often have smaller print-runs and show up only in comics-specialty stores. (260)

Graphic novels offer readers complex fantasy and science fiction stories. Shakespeare and other classics have been adapted into a graphic novel format, as have important works of autobiography and nonfiction.

In 1992, Art Speigelman won the Pulitzer Prize for *Maus*, a powerful, horrific, biographical Holocaust story based upon the experiences of Spiegelman's father, a Jew in Nazi-occupied Europe who manages to survive the Auschwitz death camp. *Maus* winning the Pulitzer Prize was a major step toward graphic novels being accepted as a serious art and literary form.

Graphic Novels Belong in Classrooms and Libraries

Graphic novels are worthy of serious consideration as legitimate art and literary art forms, but are they more than escapist entertainment? Are they only fit for leisure reading, or can graphic novels actually be the object of serious study in middle and high school classrooms? The answer is yes, and Francisa Goldsmith does an outstanding job of explaining the educational value of graphic novels:

> A literary piece that calls on its readers to use both analyzing and synthesizing skills is asking more involvement on the part of the reader, not less. Graphic novels require active, critical participation by the reader, who must not only be able to decode text but also follow its flow and grasp the essentials of narrative, mood, character, or plot through images. The reader must then be able to meld parts into a unified whole. Giving teens access to materials that help them develop their critical skills and aesthetic appreciation is part of the charge of the adult responsible for young adult collections. (1510)

Ted Hipple and Elizabeth Goza also offer a persuasive argument for including comics and graphic novels in the classroom:

> Comics combine both pictures and words in ways that often capture readers' attention, the two forms of communication blending symbiotically with text enhancing illustration and illustration enhancing text. Further, comics ARE literature in terms of its elements—characters, setting, conflicts, and so on. The major difference pedagogically between "drawn" novels and written novels, for example is the medium in which the teller tells the story. Comics do have a place in the classroom. . . . attention to comics can take on a variety of strategic forms. They can be studied as literature, with analyses of plot, character, and conflict resolutions. They can be studied as art with discussions of their illustrations. They can be studied as literature AND art, with attention to form and content. (368)

In addition to all of the wonderful pedagogical possibilities that Hipple and Goza mention, graphic novels engage and stimulate readers. Regardless of what some librarians and teachers may think, the fact is that many kids who will read nothing else will probably read comics and graphic novels. The adults who ignore this fact are missing a great opportunity to use graphic novels as a way of motivating reluctant readers to the library and read. Larry Dorrell argues that "comic books can help convince students that the library has something to offer them" (30). Stephen Weiner argues that graphic novels "should be included in the public library collection because they appeal specifically to a large reluctant patronage: teenagers" (269). Emphasizing the particular appeal graphic novels have for teens, Weiner continues: "Any librarian, upon visiting a comic book specialty shop is immediately aware that the clientele consists primarily of teenagers, and that the activities the teenagers are engaged in are reading and discussing a literature they feel pertains to them" (269). Graphic novels do have strong appeal for teenage readers, particularly males. Boys who are reluctant to read a text-only book can find an attractive alternative in graphic novels.

What makes graphic novels so appealing to teens? The short, quick, visual format of the books is attractive to a generation that has become visually oriented with media like television, computer games, and the Internet. The nonlinear narrative format of the graphic novel appeals to a generation of teens who are more accustomed to reading hypertext on a computer screen than traditional linear text. The text in word balloon bites in these stories appears to teens to be more like real conversation. The development of characters through dialogue is another appealing element. Graphic novels tend to tackle edgy themes in their stories. Graphic novels usually come in paperback format, which seems to be preferred by many teens. The fact that graphic novels come in a series is also very important. For many readers, particularly reluctant readers, the continuity and familiarity series books offer helps them become comfortable with reading and builds confidence in their ability.

Marketing Graphic Novels to Reluctant Readers

How do you get teens to come into the library to look at these books? The two main things librarians have to be conscious of is making these books as accessible and visible as possible. First of all, in the case of a public library, the books should be placed in the area or room of your library that is designated for young adults. If your library does not have such a space, put the graphic novels in the area of the library where teens are most likely to congregate. That place may be near the computers, or the reference books where they do homework, or by the magazines, depending on what your situation is. The important thing to remember is that you want these books out in an area where they will be most visible to the teens who may visit your library. In the case of a school library, the graphic novels should be put in a visible place somewhere near the entrance to draw in students who might otherwise not enter.

In both the public and school library environments, the librarian should make every effort to display the books with the covers facing out, just as bookstores and comic shops do. It is the cover that will initially draw teens to the books. You want to encourage browsing. In addition to facing covers out, you can do that by simply having a variety of titles laid out on tables, so the teens who come in and sit down will immediately pick them up and start reading.

Librarians also need to be flexible about how they classify graphic novels and where they shelve them. The public library system I worked for insisted on classifying graphic novels as art books, so they were shelved in the 700s nonfiction section. Motivated readers will look through the shelves to find these books, but reluctant readers will not. You have to make every effort to bring the books to them. If they are shelved into obscurity with the rest of the art books, or even with the rest of the fiction (assuming you have an open-minded cataloger), you are not going to grab the attention of the reluctant reader. You have to do what you can with the space available to keep the graphic novels separate and visible.

There are, of course, all the tools of the advertising and public relations trades to use in promoting your graphic novels, too. Creating and distributing promotional materials like bookmarks, handbills, or thematic bibliographies is always a good way to get attention. Local bookstores and comic shops may be willing to give you old display materials they receive from publishers.

You can also do some innovative programming to draw in potential readers. Arrange a "swap meet," in which participants bring a comic or graphic novel they are willing to trade for another. You could invite local comic shop owners to give a presentation, or if you have a local artist, invite him or her to offer a cartooning workshop. Whenever you offer programs like these, always remember to promote the books. Have them prominently on display and make sure you leave time to briefly talk about them and make your audience aware they are available to check out. You want the teens who attend these programs to not only enjoy them, but to also walk out with something to read. Never lose sight of your primary mission—getting kids to read!

Essential Graphic Novels for Your Library

Okay, so you are convinced that you should have graphic novels in your public and school library collection to attract reluctant readers, but where do you begin? The titles listed in this bibliography were selected based on what I have observed to be among the most popular of graphic novel titles with teens.

Please take note, however, that many graphic novels do contain strong adult content that would make them inappropriate for a middle school library and perhaps even high school collections. Young adult collections in public libraries have more flexibility in the content of materials housed, but use your discretion in selecting what you believe is appropriate. Graphic novels can depict nudity and graphic images of sex and violence. There are also some texts that liberally use profanity. Of the series cited below, I recommend looking closely at *The Big Book*, *Book of Magic*, *Death*, and *Sandman* series before making a purchasing decision.

Arnoldi, Katherine. *The Amazing True Adventures of a Teenage Single Mom*. New York: Hyperion, 1998.
This autobiographical story is effectively rendered in graphic novel format. A young, poor mom desperately wants to go to college, so she can make her life better for her and her baby, but she has a multitude of obstacles to overcome before she can achieve that dream. A beautifully written, poignant and moving story illustrated in black-and-white.

Avi. *City of Light, City of Dark: A Comic-Book Novel*. Illus. Brian Floc. New York: Orchard, 1993.
The first owners of Manhattan Island in New York City were Kurbs, shadowy creatures who would rent the island to humans on the condition that someone locate the source of power and return it every year to its special place. Asterel is the woman who holds this responsibility as the story unfolds, but evil Mr. Underton wants the power and charges his assistant Theo to steal it. But Theo and Asterel fall in love and marry, and Underton's plot is thwarted. This is the first attempt at a graphic novel for Avi, the author of many books for children and young adults, and he largely succeeds. It is particularly well-suited for younger adolescents.

Batman. New York: DC Comics.
Created by Bob Kane, the original Batman was a grim, menacing, vengeful character, but writers have considerably softened his image over the decades. His popularity remains high among all ages, including teens.

Titles in the series include:

Batman Archives (3 vols.)
Batman: Digital Justice
Batman: Gotham by Gaslight
Batman: The Killing Joke
Batman: Mask of the Phantasm
Batman: Master of the Future
Batman: Night Cries

Batman: No Man's Land
Batman: Tales of the Demon
Batman: The Collected Adventures (2 vols.)
Batman: The Collected Legends of the Dark Knight
Batman: The Dark Knight Returns
Batman: 3D
Batman: Venom
Batman Versus Predator
Batman: War on Crime
Batman: Year One
Batman: Year Two
The Many Deaths of Batman

Claremont, Chirs and Frank Miller. *Wolverine*. New York: Marvel
    Comics, 1992.
Wolverine is one of the most popular of the X-men characters. A
regenerating mutant, Wolverine has a skeleton of tough metal called
adamantium, keen senses, and long metal claws that shoot out from the
vicinity of his knuckles. See also the *X-Men* series.

Titles in the series include:

Wolverine
Wolverine Battles the Incredible Hulk
Wolverine: Blood Hungry
Wolverine: Bloodlust
Wolverine: Bloody Choices
Wolverine: Evilution
Wolverine/Ghost Rider: Acts of Vengance
Wolverine: Inner Fury
Wolverine/Nick Fury: The Scorpio Connection
Wolverine: Rahne of Terra
Wolverine: Save the Tiger!
Wolverine: The Jungle Adventure
Wolverine/Typhoid Mary: Typhoid's Kiss
Wolverine: Weapon X

Fleming, Robert Loren, and Robert F. Boyd, Jr. *The Big Book of Urban
    Legends*. New York: D. C. Comics.
Two hundred bizarre stories that have become part of modern
American folklore. Profanity and sexual content can be rather strong in
some the titles listed below, so I recommended them only for older teen
readers.

Other titles in *The Big Book* series (Caution: Many of these titles
contain strong adult content):

The Big Book of Conspiracies
The Big Book of Death
The Big Book of Freaks
The Big Book of Hoaxes
The Big Book of Little Criminals
The Big Book of Losers
The Big Book of Weirdos
The Big Book of the Unexplained

Gaiman, Neil. *The Book of Magic*. New York: Vertigo/D. C. Comics,
    1993.
Tim Hunter, a young boy possessed with the gift of "a natural force, for
evil, for magic or for science," is taken on a journey filled with many
emotional, moral, physical, and psychological challenges by four men
in an attempt to persuade the boy to pursue the path of magic and
goodness. This is an engrossing fantasy story exploring the classic
theme of good versus evil. The illustrations are outstanding.

Gaiman, Neil. *The Sandman*. New York: D. C. Comics.
The Sandman is an outstanding fantasy series and among Gaiman's
finest writing. The Sandman, also known as Dream, Morpheus, and a
thousand other names, is lord of the Dreaming, the place that dreaming
beings create and from which they draw their dreams. Some of the
stories center on dream, some on mortals who interact with him, and
others are retellings of myths or folktales in which Dream plays only a
minor role.

Titles in the series include:

Preludes and Nocturnes
The Doll's House
Dream Country
Seasons of Mist
A Game of You
Fables and Reflections
Brief Lives

Moore, Alan. *The Saga of the Swamp Thing*. New York: Warner, 1987.
Alec Holland, a plant biologist, turns himself into a giant plant-monster
with an experimental serum he develops. The stories are sometimes

surprisingly introspective with the character wrestling with identity issues. How much of him is human and how much plant?

O'Barr, J. *The Crow*. Northampton, MA: Kitchen Sink, 1993.
Deeply in love and engaged to be married, Eric and Shelley are brutally murdered by a thief. Eric returns from the dead as the Crow, a clown-painted immortal seeking revenge. Although not terribly deep or subtle, this is an immensely popular revenge fantasy thanks in large part to the success of the motion picture based upon the book.

Smith, Jeff. *The Complete Bone Adventures*. Los Gatos, CA: Cartoon Books, 1993-1994. 3 vols.
One of the most popular comics of the 1990s, Bone is about two cousins, Fone and Smiley Bone, who help their cousin, Phoney Bone, escape the angry citizens of Boneville. The three find themselves in all sorts of bizarre, zany predicaments and adventures. The author relies on dialogue to carry the story. There is plenty of humor that is surprisingly subtle and sometimes quite sophisticated. The art is also deceptively simple. An entertaining title readers of all ages will appreciate.

Spider-Man. New York: Marvel Comics.
After the X-Men, Spider-Man is among the most popular superheroes with adolescent readers. A few titles from the series are a must for a collection of any size.

Titles in *The Amazing Spider-Man* series include:

The Amazing Spider-Man
The Death of Jean De Wolff
Fearful Symmetry: Kraven's Last Hunt
Hooky
The Origin of the Hobgoblin
Parallel Lives
The Saga of the Alien Costume
Spirits of the Dead
Torment
The Wedding

Titles in the *Spider-Man* series include:

The Assassin Nation Plot
Carnage
The Cosmic Adventures

Fear Itself
His Greatest Team-Up Battles
The Origin of the Hobgoblin
The Secret Story of Marvel's World Famous Wall-Crawler
Venom Returns

Titles in which Spider-Man teams up with other Marvel Characters:

Spider-Man, Punisher, Sabre-Tooth: Designer Genes
Spider-Man/Dr. Strange: The Way to Dusty Death
X-Force and Spider-Man: Sabotage

Spiegelman, Art. *Maus: A Survivor's Tale. Part I: My Father Bleeds
   History.* New York: Pantheon, 1986.
A biographical account of Spiegelman's father, a Holocaust survivor,
told in a graphic novel format. Spiegelman portrays Nazis as cats and
Jews as mice. The author depicts himself being told about the
Holocaust by his Polish father. The story explores a troubled
relationship between father and son, as well as the concentration camp
experience. The story and black-and-white illustrations are grim and
powerful.

Spiegelman, Art. *Maus: A Survivor's Tale: Part II: And Here My
   Troubles Began.* New York: Pantheon, 1991.
Spiegelman continues the story of his father's Holocaust experiences in
the same graphic novel format. In this book, the father's Auschwitz
experiences are depicted in his life after liberation. A powerful, horrific
book and an outstanding sequel.

Superman. New York: D. C. Comics.
Perhaps the most important figure in comic book history, Superman
does not seem as popular as fellow superheroes Batman, Spiderman,
and X-Men, but he does have a significant following among
contemporary teen readers.

Titles in the series include:

The Greatest Superman Stories Ever Told
Superman Archives
Superman: Panic in the Sky
Superman: Peace on Earth
Superman: Speeding Bullets
Superman: The Earth Stealers

Superman: The Man of Steel
Superman: Time and Again

See also *The Death of Superman* series:

The Death of Superman
Return of Superman
World Without a Superman

Tolkien, J. R. R. *The Hobbit, or There and Back*. Adapted by Charles
Dixon. Illus. David Wenzel. New York: Ballantine, 1990.
An abridgement of the original text. Wenzel's depitction of Gollum is
wonderfully grotesque. This book is a great means of tuning reluctant
readers on to Tolkien.

Winick, Judd. *Pedro and Me: Friendship, Loss, and What I Learned*.
New York: Holt, 2000.
For five months in 1994, Pedro Zamora, a young HIV-positive AIDS
educator, lived with six other people in a house in San Francisco to be
filmed for the popular MTV series *The Real World*. One of the people
living with Pedro, the author became a close friend and was deeply
affected when Pedro finally succumbed to AIDS. Winick's story, told
in graphic novel format with black-and-white illustrations, recounts
their meeting, the friendship that evolved, and how Pedro's death
affected his life. The story occasionally becomes emotionally
overwrought to the point of becoming shallow, but ultimately it is quite
memorable and moving.

X-Men. New York: Marvel Comics.
Teenage mutant superheroes battling the forces of evil. Need I say
more? There is no denying this series is enormously popular and, with
the popularity of the animated series and the successful, recently
released motion picture, it is unlikely the popularity will fade anytime
soon. This series is one of the most popular among adolescent boys I
worked with in Staten Island. See also *Wolverine* series.

The series includes these titles:

The X-Men
The X-Men Adventures
X-Men: The Asgardian Wars
X-Men: The Dark Phoenix Saga
X-Men: Days of Future Past

X-Men: Days of Future Present
X-Men: From the Ashes
X-Men: God Loves, Man Kills
X-Men: Savage Land
X-Men: X-tinction Agenda
X-Men vs. the Avengers
X-Men vs. Brood

Keeping Current with Graphic Novels

Graphic novels are unfortunately not regularly or widely reviewed in professional journals used by librarians as selection guides. Katherine "Kat" Kan writes the indispensable "Graphically Speaking" review column, which first appeared in *VOYA: Voice of Youth Advocates* in the February 1994 issue and continues to appear in every other issue of the bi-monthly journal. In each column, Kan discusses developments in one or more graphic novel series. Reviews of individual titles occasionally appear in *Booklist*, *School Library Journal*, and *VOYA*, but there is currently no comprehensive review venue for librarians to consult. Another helpful source for discussion and information is the "Graphic Novels in Libraries" electronic discussion list. The purpose of the discussion list is to "share reviews and resources for collection development of your graphic or comic novel section." To join the list, send an e-mail to GNLIB-L-subscribe@topica.com.

Directory of Comic and Graphic Novel Publishers

Dark Horse Comics
10956 SE Main Street
Milwaukie, OR 97222
http://www.darkhorse.com

DC Comics
1700 Broadway
New York, NY 10019
(800) 887-6789
DCOSubs@aol.com
http://www.dccomics.com

Kitchen Sink Press
320 Riverside Drive
Northampton, MA 01060

(800) 365-7465
kitchensp@aol.com

Marvel Entertainment Group, Inc.
387 Park Avenue South
New York, NY 10016
(212) 696-0808
mail@marvel.com
http://www.marvel.com

Works Cited

Barron, Daniel D. "Zap! Pow! Wham!: Comics, Graphic Novels, and Education." *School Library Media Activities Monthly* 8 (November 1991): 48-50.

DeCandido, Keith R. A. "Picture This: Graphic Novels in Libraries." *Library Journal* 115 (March 15, 1990): 50-55.

Dorrell, Larry D. "Why Comic Books?" *School Library Journal* (November 1987): 30-32.

Dorrell, Larry D., and C. Edward Carroll. "Spiderman at the Library." *School Library Journal* 27.10 (August 1981): 118-120.

Ellman, Neil. "Comics in the Classroom." *Audiovisual Instructor* 24.5 (May 1979): 24-25.

Freeman, Matt. "The Case for Comics." *Reading Today* 15.3 (December 1997/January 1998): 3-5.

Gagnier, S. Richard. "A Hunger for Heroes." *School Library Journal* (September 1997): 143.

Goldsmith, Francisca. "YA Talk: Graphic Novels." *Booklist* 94.17 (May 1, 1998): 1510-1511.

Hipple, Ted, and Elizabeth Goza. "It Ain't Only Books Any More." *Into Focus: Understanding and Creating Middle School Readers.* Eds. Kylene Beers and Barbara G. Samuels. Norwood, MA: Christopher-Gordon, 1998.

Kan, Katherine L. "Comics and Graphic Novels in the Library." *Voice of Youth Advocates* 22.4 (October 1999): 252-253.

Reid, Calvin. "Picture This." *Publishers Weekly* (October 12, 1990): 17-20.

Rothschild, D. Aviva. *Graphic Novels: A Bibliographic Guide to Book-Length Comics.* Englewood, CO: Libraries Unlimited, 1995. (1-56308-086-9)

Sherman, Gale W., and Bette D. Ammon. "Beyond Superman: The Boom in Trade Comics." *School Library Journal* 39 (May 1993): 34-35.

Spiegelman, Art. *Maus I: A Survivor's Tale: My Father Bleeds History.* New York: Pantheon, 1986.

———. *Maus II: A Survivor's Tale: And Here My Troubles Began.* New York: Pantheon, 1991.

Swain, Emma Halstead. "Using Comic Books to Teach Reading and Language Arts." *Journal of Reading* 22.3 (December 1978): 253-258.

Weiner, Stephen. "Creating a Graphics Novel Collection for the Public Library." *Voice of Youth Advocates* 15.5 (December 1992): 269-270, 272.

Wright, Gary. "The Comic Book—A Forgotten Medium in the Classroom." *The Reading Teacher* 33.2 (November 1979): 158-161.

Chapter 5
Resources for Reluctant Readers: Nonfiction

Nonfiction just doesn't get any respect from librarians and teachers. Middle and high school students come into the public library with reading lists assigned by their English teachers and nowhere, among dozens of choices, is a single nonfiction title. On those rare occasions when a student does come in with a more inclusive list, it is still disproportionately skewed toward fiction. On the shelves of paperbacks teachers have for self-selected reading, there are few, if any, nonfiction titles. Why is it that so many educators do not hold nonfiction in high regard? Why this propensity to be "fictioncentric"? When librarians and teachers think of literature, they typically think of fiction. Penny Colman, a distinguished author of many nonfiction books for young adults, laments at how many librarians and teachers have told her that reading nonfiction is not "real reading" (215). In other words, not much, if any, literary value is accorded to nonfiction books. Richard Abrahamson and Betty Carter (1998) observe: "One of the most prevalent misconceptions about the role of nonfiction in the lives of young teens is that they read nonfiction just to aid them in homework assignments. It's just not true" (315). Many educators think of nonfiction as informational; something to be used for homework assignments. What happens, then, is that a lot of adolescents who would read nonfiction with interest and enthusiasm are disenfranchised.

In reviews of nonfiction books, I consistently see reviewers comments about the author's thoroughness in addressing the subject, the organization and layout of the information, the ease with which the information is accessible, if there is a glossary and index, and other observations about the book's overall usefulness. Rarely does a nonfiction review go beyond the superficial, offering commentary about the aesthetic qualities of the book: the author's ability to craft an engaging narrative, its structure, point of view, pace, tone, voice, and so on. Rarely is any speculation made about how pleasurable a reader may find the text, as if it is impossible to actually *enjoy* reading nonfiction.

Nonfiction is regarded in purely utilitarian terms. A book's merits are judged exclusively upon its usefulness to the reader. It does not seem to occur to some educators that nonfiction can simply be a "good read"; something entertaining, fun, enjoyable, or just plain interesting. Carter and Abrahamson (1990) note: "Much of the nonfiction read by young adults is read for pleasure, diversion, and entertainment" (8). Many young adults do actually prefer to read such books. I preferred reading nonfiction as a teen and still do as an adult. Discussing two reading studies in 1972 and 1973, Carter and Abrahamson (1990) state: "Nonfiction becomes an increasingly important component in overall reading preferences as young adults mature" (4). English teachers should remember that nonfiction is the preferred reading choice of many of their students. Abrahamson and Carter (1993) note in their study of reading preferences of young adults: "What we know is that young adults in the middle and high schools of America make nonfiction books a substantial part of their self-selected reading. . . . Educators must first of all recognize and reward the nonfiction reading that teens do just as they praise their reading of fiction" (167). Teachers can capitalize on this interest in nonfiction and get their students really excited about reading.

Colman (1999) believes there are at least three reasons why negative perceptions of nonfiction persist. The first is that in the world of publishing for youth, the personal preferences of influential editors, educators, librarians, and reviewers for fiction has a profound impact. The second is the romanticized image adults have for children's and young adult fiction. The third reason is Zena Sutherland's coining of the term *informational books* for nonfiction, which unfortunately caught on and continues to shape how people in education, librarianship, and publishing view it (216-217). Nonfiction is not just about information. The truth is that, for many young adult readers, nonfiction serves the same purposes as fiction does for other readers: it entertains, provides escape, sparks the imagination, and indulges curiosity. There's a lot more to a good nonfiction book than mere information.

One example of superior nonfiction that can appeal to many reluctant readers is Jennifer Armstrong's *Shipwreck at the Bottom of the World*. Armstrong chronicles the ordeal of Sir Ernest Shackleton's ill-fated expedition to Antarctica aboard the *Endurance* in 1914. The explorer's goal was to be the first to cross the continent. The expedition was doomed to failure. Before reaching the continent, the ship became trapped in ice and was soon crushed to pieces. Shackleton and his crew were left stranded in the Antarctic wasteland for nineteen months, living in camps constructed from the ruins of their ship on ice floes. They would have to endure two hundred mile per hour winds and temperatures well below zero Fahrenheit. After five months of moving from one ice floe to another, Shackleton and his men made a daring, perilous escape in three tiny, open lifeboats hundreds of miles to the uninhabited Elephant Island. From there, Shackleton and five crewman left in one of the lifeboats on an eight hundred mile open boat journey though treacherous seas to reach South Georgia Island where the only human inhabitants were the employees of a whaling station. Shackleton and his men reached the other side of the island safely, only to have to scale ice-covered, uncharted mountains to reach the whaling station. It would be months more before the crew left behind on Elephant Island could be rescued. Miraculously, every member of the expedition survived.

This extraordinary true story of adventure and survival is one that authors like Will Hobbs or Gary Paulsen could not begin to imagine in their fiction. More than an adventure story, *Shipwreck at the Bottom of the World* is a spellbinding, inspirational tale of extraordinary leadership and ingenuity, of the triumph of the human spirit in the face of overwhelming adversities, of camaraderie, devotion, and loyalty. Armstrong takes the facts of the event and weaves them into an engaging, enthralling human drama that is as rich in themes, conflicts, and memorable characters as any work of fiction. She achieves this by bringing a wonderful authenticity to the narrative through the frequent quotations of primary sources, such as the log entries of Captain Frank Worsley, and the personal accounts written by Shackleton and members of the expedition. Complementing the text are extraordinary photographs taken by expedition photographer Frank Hurley, who was able to chronicle the entire ordeal. Readers are treated to both a stunning visual and written account. *Shipwreck at the Bottom of the World* exemplifies all those qualities that make for outstanding nonfiction. It simply does not get any better. Regrettably, books like *Shipwreck at the Bottom of the World* are the exception rather than the rule in young adult nonfiction publishing these days.

Unfortunately, a lot of poor quality nonfiction is being published these days that perpetuates the misconception that nonfiction is just about information. Publishers specializing in series books are in the business of cranking out nonfiction in assembly-like fashion for school libraries and classrooms. What these publishers typically do is find a subject that they can milk for all it's worth, producing brief, superficial, poorly designed, cheaply made, and outrageously overpriced books. These types of series nonfiction books consistently feature awful cover designs, didactic and dull writing, unimaginative layout and design of text and illustrations, and repetitive use of stock photographs that do little to complement the text. Information in these books is "dumbed down" for the reader, in the same way that textbooks manage to strip facts down to the most unappealing presentation imaginable.

These books may indeed inform the reader, often condescendingly, but they do nothing to engage the mind or spark the imagination. They certainly do not reflect a respect for their audience. They succeed only in reducing reading to a boring, laborious chore. It is not the concept of series to which I object. I do not agree that because a book is part of a series that it cannot be one of quality and substance. The reality, however, is that many series books, particularly nonfiction series books, are too often sub-standard in quality and substance, and that libraries and schools are charged exorbitant amounts of money for these inferior products. It is these types of books that perpetuate the image of young adult nonfiction as only "informational" books—books only to be used, not enjoyed.

Another reason why teachers may not value nonfiction has to do with the fact that they may not understand how to use it with their students. Unrecognized is the potential nonfiction has to stimulate the analytical and critical thinking skills found in fiction. Abrahamson and Carter (1993) observe that educators are uncomfortable with nonfiction because they do not know how to approach it. They note: "There are many reasons why educators do not value the nonfiction reading their students do as much as they value their fiction reading. Perhaps teachers and librarians unconsciously perpetuate a bias toward fiction because nonfiction was not stressed in their own course of study" (168). Teachers know how to ask questions of fiction readers dealing with such elements as characterization, conflict, point of view, setting, theme, and so on, but they are often at a loss as to what to do with nonfiction. In their book, *Nonfiction for Young Adults: From Delight to Wisdom*, Carter and Abrahamson suggest ten questions educators can use as a basis for designing strategies to elicit student responses about nonfiction. The questions address such factors as: the context of the time in which the book was written; the role illustrations play in the book, and how they do or do not successfully complement the text; the quality of the book as compared to others written on the same topic; which part, if any, of the book might make a good documentary film; the depth of research the author employed to write the book; the success of the book in speaking to its intended audience, and how it would be altered to speak to a different audience; how the author succeeds in teaching the reader about his/her subject; what the reader would ask the author about the book in an interview; what facts or ideas found in the book would the reader want to further investigate; and how the cover art and title of the book effectively represent its contents (186-187). Good nonfiction books are as rich in possibilities for deep, thoughtful discussion as any good novel.

There are a significant number of teens who prefer "the real thing" for their reading. Teachers can incorporate a variety of nonfiction titles in reading lists to encourage students to make nonfiction a significant part of their self-selected reading diet. Carter and Abrahamson (1993) note: "The middle school years are the time when nonfiction reading can flourish if teachers and librarians encourage and value these books. For many middle school youngsters, nonfiction will be the vehicle that will take them down the highway of lifetime reading" (329).

Twenty-Five Nonfiction Titles for Reluctant Readers

Armstrong, Jennifer. *Shipwreck at the Bottom of the World: The Extraordinary True Story of Shackleton and the Endurance.* New York: Crown, 1998.
A superbly written account of Sir Ernest Shackleton's ill-fated expedition to the Antarctic aboard the *Endurance* in 1914. The text is abundantly illustrated with crew member Frank Hurley's astonishing photographs chronicling the ordeal. This riveting account of the expedition is particularly well suited for middle school audiences.

Bode, Janet and Stan Mack. *Heartbreak and Roses: Real Life Stories of Troubled Love.* New York: Delacorte, 1994.
An outstanding collection of voices of teenagers talking about their experiences with obsessive love, tormented love, bittersweet love, and other kinds of heartbreak. Readers will find these stories both compelling and comforting. There are many other nonfiction titles by the late Janet Bode (most in collaboration with Stan Mack) that will appeal to reluctant young adult readers, including: *Death Is Hard to Live With: Teenagers Talk about How They Cope with Loss* (Delacorte, 1993); Hard *Time: A Real Life Look at Juvenile Crime and Violence* (Delacorte, 1996); and *Trust and Betrayal: Real Life Stories of Friends and Enemies* (Delacorte, 1995).

Colman, Penny. *Corpses, Coffins, and Crypts: A History of Burial.* New York: Henry Holt, 1997.
The ways in which people from different cultures and different times deal with death is documented through lively, fast-paced narrative and many contemporary and historical black-and-white photographs.

————. *Toilets, Bathtubs, Sinks and Sewers: A History of the Bathroom.* New York: Atheneum, 1994.
A wonderful, entertaining chronicle of the history of bathrooms from ancient times to the present.

Deem, James M. *Bodies from the Bog*. Boston: Houghton Mifflin, 1998.
A fascinating discussion of the discovery in northern Europe of remarkably preserved bog bodies thousands of years old. The lively text is complemented throughout with illustrations, many of which are quite grotesque photographs of discovered remains.

Elffers, Joost, and Saxton Freymann. *Play With Your Food*. 1997. New York: Stewart, Tabori & Chang.
A delightful, whimsical collection of vegetable creatures presented in glorious color photographs. Includes step-by-step instructions for readers who wish to create their own creatures.

Farrell, Jeanette. *Invisible Enemies: Stories of Infectious Diseases*. New York: Farrar Straus Giroux, 1998.
An engrossing account of seven deadly diseases (AIDS, bubonic plague, cholera, leprosy, malaria, smallpox, and tuberculosis) that have ravaged humankind through the ages.

Feelings, Tom. *The Middle Passage: White Ships/Black Cargo*. New York: Dial, 1995.
A profoundly moving chronicle of the cruel, terrifying journey of enslaved Africans across the Atlantic Ocean rendered in wordless, black-and-white illustrations. The illustrations are intensely emotional, haunting, and horrific. An introduction by Dr. John Henrik Clarke offers excellent historical background on the African slave trade.

Freedman, Russell. *Martha Graham: A Dancer's Life*. New York: Clarion, 1998.
A lusciously illustrated and lovingly written biography of the mother of modern dance.

Gaskins, Pearl Fuyo. *What Are You? Voices of Mixed-Race Young People*. New York: Holt, 1999.
An insightful collection of interviews with eighty mixed-race young people discussing, in their own words, the many issues they face like dating, family life, prejudice, and struggles with their identity.

Giblin, James Cross. *Charles A. Lindbergh: A Human Hero*. New York: Clarion, 1997.
A highly readable, well-rounded account of the aviator's extraordinary and controversial life.

Kerr, M. E. *Blood on the Forehead: What I Know about Writing*. New
    York: HarperCollins, 1998.
This pioneer of young adult literature offers readers insights into how
authors get their ideas and craft successful stories.

Krull, Kathleen. *Lives of the Writers: Comedies, Tragedies (and What
    the Neighbors Thought)*. San Diego: Harcourt Brace, 1994.
Twenty humorous, sometimes hilarious, brief portraits of writers like
Charlotte Bronte, Charles Dickens, Langston Hughes, and Mark Twain
are accompanied with caricature illustrations. Entertaining, but also
quite informative. Other books in the same format by the same author
and illustrator include: *Lives of the Artists, Lives of the Athletes, Lives
of the Musicians*, and *Lives of the Presidents* (Harcourt Brace, 1998).

Lawlor, Laurie. *Where Will This Shoe Take You?: A Walk through the
    History of Footwear*. New York: Walker, 1996.
A history of footwear from woven bark to Air Jordans is presented in a
lively, straightforward narrative complemented throughout by lots of
black-and-white illustrations.

Macaulay, David. *The New Way Things Work*. Boston: Houghton
    Mifflin, 1998.
An expanded and updated edition of the incredibly brilliant and highly
original guide to the inner workings of machines of all kinds. From
very simple tools to mind-boggling, complex technologies, Macaulay
explains all the intricacies of these devices through engaging text and
astonishingly detailed illustrations.

Macy, Sue. *Winning Ways: A Photohistory of American Women in
    Sports*. New York: Holt, 1996.
A marvelous celebration of the exploits of female athletes like Babe
Didrikson, Althea Gibson, and Martina Navratilova. In addition to
profiling women in sports, going back to the 1800s, Macy also
discusses the controversies surrounding their participation. Fast-paced,
well-written, and abundantly illustrated throughout.

Marrin, Albert. *Terror of the Spanish Main: Sir Henry Morgan and His
    Buccaneers*. New York: Dutton, 1999.
A compelling history of New World buccaneers and Sir Henry Morgan,
one of their famous leaders.

Mastoon, Adam. *The Shared Heart: Portraits and Stories Celebrating Lesbian, Gay, and Bisexual Young People*. New York: Morrow, 1997.
An outstanding collection of forty frank, open narratives and photographs of gay, lesbian, and bisexual young adults ranging in age from late teens to early twenties, telling what it is like to be bisexual and homosexual.

McKissack, Patricia C. and Frederick L. McKissack. *Young, Black, and Determined: A Biography of Lorraine Hansberry*. New York: Holiday House, 1998.
An intense, involving chronicle of the life of the successful African-American playwright. Attractively illustrated with many black-and-white photographs.

Murphy, Jim. *Gone A-Whaling: The Lure of the Sea and the Hunt for the Great Whale*. New York: Clarion, 1998.
The history of American whaling brought vividly to life through an engrossing narrative that is frequently drawn from firsthand accounts in diaries, letters, and journals of young men who signed on to whaling voyages.

Patridge, Elizabeth. *Restless Spirit: The Life and Work of Dorothea Lange*. New York: Viking, 1998.
An exceptional biography of the influential photographer who chronicled such subjects as the living conditions of migrant workers, Japanese American internees, and rural poverty. Handsomely illustrated with many of Lange's stunning black-and-white photographs.

Spinelli, Jerry. *Knots in My Yo-yo String: The Autobiography of a Kid*. New York: Knopf, 1998.
This is a charming reminiscence of the young adult author's childhood growing up in rural Pennsylvania, but reluctant readers will find of most interest Spinelli's own trouble in school and learning to read.

Thomas, Velma Maia. *Lest We Forget: The Passage from Africa to Slavery and Emancipation*. New York: Crown, 1997.
Featuring documents and photographs from the Black Holocaust Exhibit in Atlanta, this outstanding three-dimensional interactive book chronicles the enslavement of Africans in America.

Ungerer, Tomi. *Tomi: A Childhood under the Nazis*. Boulder, CO: Roberts Rinehart, 1998.

Alsatian artist Tomi Ungerer offers an extraordinary personal look at what it was like to live under Nazi occupation. Complementing Ungerer's own words and images are dozens of rare artifacts and documents produced by the Nazi propaganda machine: children's books, decrees, pamphlets, photographs, postcards, posters, school textbooks, songbooks, and toys. The result is a stunning visual memoir, a kind of museum in a book.

Wooldridge, Susan G. *Poemcrazy: Freeing Your Life with Words*. New York: Potter, 1996.
Much more than a manual on how to read and write a poem, Wooldridge's infectious, unbridled enthusiasm for poetry will inspire even the most devoted hater of poetry to start reading and writing verse.

Works Cited

Abrahamson, Richard F., and Betty Carter. "What We Know about Nonfiction and Young Adult Readers and What We Need to Do about It." *Inspiring Literacy: Literature for Children and Young Adults*. Eds. Sam Sebesta and Ken Donelson. New Brunswick, NJ: Transaction, 1993.

Carter, Betty, and Richard F. Abrahamson. "Castles to Colin Powell: The Truth about Nonfiction." *Into Focus: Understanding and Creating Middle School Readers*. Eds. Kylene Beers and Barbara G. Samuels. Norwood, MA: Christopher-Gordon, 1998.

————. *Nonfiction for Young Adults: From Delight to Wisdom*. Phoenix, AZ: Oryx, 1990.

————. "Nonfiction in a Read-Aloud Program." *Journal of Reading* 34.8 (May 1991): 638-642.

Colman, Penny. "Nonfiction Is Literature, Too." *The New Advocate* 12.3 (Summer 1999): 215-223.

Sullivan, Ed. "Some Teens Prefer It Real: The Case for Young Adult Nonfiction." *English Journal* 90.3 (January 2001): 43-47.

Chapter 6
Resources for Reluctant Readers: Picture Books

Picture Books Are NOT for Children Only

Since so many teachers will dismiss all adolescent literature outright as "sub-literature," resistance to using picture books in the classroom should come as no surprise. Most people have the erroneous notion that picture books are appropriate only for young children. This is unfortunate because many of the picture books that are published every year, perhaps a majority of them, are completely inappropriate for young children because the complexity and sophistication of the art and text in these books are lost on that audience. They cannot appreciate or understand these stories.

One need only to look at recent Caldecott Medal-winning books to see how sophisticated picture books can be. The Caledcott medal is an annual award given by the Association of Library Services for Children, a division of the American Library Association, to the most distinguished picture book published in a given year. In 1982 the winning title was Nancy Willard's *A Visit to William Blake's Inn: Poems for Innocent and Experienced Travelers*, a beautifully illustrated collection of eighteen original lyrical and nonsensical poems written as a tribute to the eighteenth-century English poet and artist William Blake. Is that the sort of book that can be appreciated by elementary school children? Hardly, but a creative high school English teacher could use this book to introduce students to a lesson on Blake's own poetry or English Romanticism.

The 1995 Caledcott winner, *Smoky Night*, written by Eve Bunting and illustrated by David Diazand, tells the story of a family living through the destructive and deadly riots that erupted in Los Angeles following the acquittal of police officers who were charged with using excessive force against Rodney King in an arrest. Again, this is a story far more likely to be appreciated by an older audience who can understand complex issues like injustice, racism, and rioting. Teachers can use this book to preface a lesson on any of those subjects. Picture books are varied enough in subject matter and theme to be used across the curriculum. *Math Curse* by Jon Scieszka and Lane Smith, for example, tells the hilarious story of a "mathphobic" boy haunted by decimals and fractions. A math teacher could use this book to help the anxieties of students dreading a new unit.

What Is a Picture Book?

Traditionally, a picture book is defined as a story that is told through the blending of text and visual art. The pictures and text work interdependently to tell the story. This is an important distinction from an illustrated book. Picture books are sometimes erroneously called illustrated books. In an illustrated book, the art exists simply to complement the text. Bette Ammon and Gale Sherman offer a good explanation of the role of art in a picture book: "The art in these books doesn't merely visualize what the words are saying; instead it goes beyond, giving readers more depth of meaning to the text" (ix). Picture books are typically thirty-two pages long, but they can vary in length from twenty-four to sixty-four pages. Illustrations can occupy one page or may have a double page spread. They may appear on a page with text or separately. The textual content in a picture book is typically brief. There is also a growing body of wordless picture books. Picture books span all literary genres: biography, fiction, folklore, nonfiction, and poetry. Sub-genres that are specific to picture books include alphabet books, concept books, counting books, and pop-ups. These types of books are generally geared for younger audiences, but older audiences can even find enjoyment in the intricacies of many of these titles.

Why Use Picture Books with Reluctant Readers?

The many competitors against reading, like computer games, the Internet, and television, are highly visual media. The constant use of this media has helped develop in adolescents sophisticated comprehension skills for visual and nonlinear narratives. In addition to those attributes is the appeal of brevity. At thirty-two or even sixty-four pages, reading a book of this kind is far less intimidating to a reluctant reader. The ability to be able to read an entire book in one sitting can inspire a great deal of confidence in a student who is completely unconfident about reading.

Twenty-Five Picture Books with Young Adult Appeal

Bunting, Eve. *Terrible Things*. Illus. Stephen Gansmell. New York: Harper & Row, 1980.
A picture book based upon Pastor Martin Niemöller's statement: "In Germany, they came first for the communists, and I didn't speak up because I wasn't a communist. Then they came for the Jews, and I didn't speak up because I wasn't a Jew. Then they came for the trade unionists, and I didn't speak up because I wasn't a trade unionist. Then they came for the Catholics and I didn't speak up because I wasn't a Catholic. Then they came for me—and by that time there was no one left to speak up." Bunting creates a fascinating story about animals in the forest who are taken away by the Terrible Things. Big Rabbit finds reasons for each of these "round-ups" until the rabbits are all that are left in the forest and the Terrible Things come for them too. This is a great book to use an introduction to a lesson on the Holocaust, or any lesson teaching the necessity of compassion toward others.

Curry, Barbara K., and James Michael Brodie. *Sweet Words So Brave: The Story of African-American Literature*. Illus. Jerry Butler. Madison, WI: Zino, 1996.
An abbreviated but informative history of African-American literature from slave narratives to the present.

Dillon, Leo, and Diane Dillon. *To Everything There Is a Season*. New York: Scholastic, 1998.
A gorgeously illustrated rendering of the well-known verses from the *Book of Ecclesiastes*. The book features elegant paintings derived from many periods in history and from many world cultures. This is a wonderful book for art teachers to use to introduce students to art styles from many diverse cultures.

Granfield, Linda. *In Flanders Field: The Story of the Poem by John McCrae*. Illus. Janet Wilson. New York: Doubleday, 1996.
A unique book that combines the famous poem with biographical information about McCrae and shows its historical context though wartime artifacts and conditions. There is great potential use here for both English and history teachers.

Hodges, Margaret. *Saint George and the Dragon*. Illus. Trina Schart Hyman. Boston: Little, Brown, 1984.
The Red Cross Knight slays a fearsome dragon. Introduce a lesson on medieval times with this book, or a lesson on folklore.

Larson, Gary. *There's a Hair in My Dirt: A Worm's Story*. New York: HarperCollins, 1998.
A sound ecological message comes through in this zany, often hilarious story from the creator of *The Far Side* comic strip. The book provides a great opportunity for science teachers to bring some levity into their lesson.

Lester, Julius. *From Slave Ship to Freedom Road*. Illus. Rod Brown. New York: Dial, 1998.
Lester's profound, passionate, and provocative meditations on slavery are perfectly complemented with Brown's striking illustrations. An outstanding introduction to the subject for a history class.

Lorbiecki, Marybeth. *Just One Flick of a Finger*. Illus. David Diaz. New York: Dial, 1996.
The all-too topical theme of guns and violence in schools is explored in this story rendered in unevenly effective hip-hop rhyme and illustrated in stunning fluorescent art. Sometimes overly moralistic, the book works overall. Counselors and teachers can use this as a springboard for discussions on defusing violent behavior and resolving conflicts.

Macaulay, David. *Baaaa*. Boston: Houghton Mifflin, 1985.
Sheep take over when the last human being disappears from the earth, but they too eventually vanish when they repeat the same mistakes as humankind. This story is a great introduction to allegory, a literary concept that is difficult for many students to understand. Read this story aloud as a prelude to studying Nathaniel Hawthorne's short stories.

Macaulay, David. *Black and White*. Boston: Houghton Mifflin, 1990.
Four stories work both independently and together as people, trains, cows, newspapers, and humor interact and intertwine in a nonlinear narrative. A great book to use to examine multiple perspectives and narrative structure.

Maruki, Toshi. *Hiroshima No Pika*. New York: Lothrop, Lee and Shepard, 1980.
A mother recounts what happened to her family during the flash that destroyed Hiroshima in 1945. A book full of unforgettable horrific images.

McDermott, Gerald. *Arrow to the Sun: A Pueblo Indian Tale*. Harcourt Brace Jovanovich, 1974.

A retelling of an ancient Pueblo Indian myth in which a young man sets out to prove he is the son and spirit of the Lord of the Sun. A great introduction to mythology or Native American studies.

Polacco, Patricia. *Pink and Say*. New York: Philomel, 1994.
Say Curtis, a Union solider left for dead, is rescued by Pinkus, a Black soldier separated from his regiment. A wonderful story of friendship and an excellent companion for a unit on the Civil War.

Raschka, Chris. *Arlene Sardine*. New York: Orchard, 1998.
The brief life of Arlene, from live brisling to canned sardine is told in this darkly humorous tale. Teachers can have fun using this book to introduce their students to irony and black comedy. This is a good prelude to Jonathan Swift's "A Modest Proposal," which so many literal-minded high school students take seriously.

Scieszka, Jon. *Math Curse*. Illus. Lane Smith. New York: Viking, 1995.
A boy is tormented by the math problems he constantly sees popping up in everyday things. A humorous story to which any student who has problems with math can relate. Math teachers can interject some levity into class reading this aloud.

Scieszka, Jon. *The Stinky Cheese Man and Other Fairly Stupid Tales*. Illus. Lane Smith. New York: Viking, 1992.
This is a hilarious collection of eleven "fractured" retellings of well-known fairy tales like "Rumplestiltskin" and "The Ugly Duckling." An excellent device for introducing students to the difficult literary concepts of parody and satire.

Scieszka, Jon. *The True Story of the Three Little Pigs*. Illus. Lane Smith. New York: Viking, 1989.
Alexander T. Wolf tells his side of the story in this "fractured" retelling of the "The Three Little Pigs." Like *The Stinky Cheese Man* collection, this is another excellent books to use to introduce students to satire, as well as point of view.

Sis, Peter. *Starry Messenger*. New York: Farrar Straus Giroux, 1996.
A strikingly handsome book depicting the life of Galileo Galilei. Science teachers can begin a unit on astronomy by sharing this book with students.

Taylor, Clark. *The House that Crack Built.* Illus. Jan Thompson Dicks. San Francisco: Chronicle, 1992.

The familiar childhood rhyme "The House that Jack Built" is used to present a powerful look at crack cocaine and its terrible impact on society. Drug counselors can use this is as a powerful way of getting the message across.

Tsuchiya, Yukio. *Faithful Elephants: A True Story of Animals, People, and War.* Trans. Tomoko Tsuchiya Dykes. Illus. Ted Lewin. Boston: Houghton Mifflin, 1988.

The heartbreaking, tragic story of John, Tonky, and Wally, three elephants at Ueno Zoo who had to be killed because of the danger of their escape during bombing raids. Although the historical accuracy of the title has been recently called into question, the story remains a powerful depiction of the horrors of war.

Van Allsburg, Chris. *The Mysteries of Harris Burdick.* Boston: Houghton Mifflin, 1984.

Brief, provocative text accompany fourteen mysterious paintings. Another good title to use in a lesson on perspective.

Van Allsburg, Chris. *The Widow's Broom.* Boston: Houghton Mifflin, 1992.

A witch discards an old broom, but the widow Minna Shaw finds it still has some magic left. The broom, however, does some magic of its own which brings big trouble to neighbors and villagers. An art teacher can use this book to show students how effectively mood is conveyed through illustrations.

Wiesner, David. *Tuesday.* New York: Clarion, 1991.

A wordless picture book in which frogs mysteriously and inexplicably begin flying through the air on their lily pads. A bizarre, stunning story that will provoke plenty of discussion. Encourage students to write text to accompany the story.

Willard, Nancy. *A Visit to William Blake's Inn: Poems for Innocent and Experienced Travelers.* Illus. Alice Provensen and Martin Provensen. San Diego: Harcourt Brace Jovanovich, 1981.

A beautifully illustrated collection of eighteen original lyrical and nonsensical poems written as a tribute to the eighteenth century English poet and artist William Blake. High school English teachers can use this book to introduce students to a lesson on Blake's own poetry or English Romanticism.

Willard, Nancy. *Pish Posh, Said Hieronymous Bosch*. Illus. Leo Dillon, and Diane Dillon. Harcourt Brace, 1991.
This book is as outrageous and surreal as Bosch's own paintings. It is sure to spark the imagination of readers and inspire them to look closely at Bosch's work.

Works Cited

Ammon, Bette D., and Gale Sherman. *Worth a Thousand Words: Picture Books for Older Readers*. Englewood, CO: Libraries Unlimited, 1996.

Chapter 7
Resources for Reluctant Readers: Magazines

All teenagers are drawn to magazines. Reluctant readers who refuse to read everything else will look at magazines. They may not read the articles, but at least the act of browsing through them, looking at the illustrations, perhaps reading the accompanying captions, is better than reading nothing at all. Magazines are one of the best weapons against aliteracy for a variety of reasons. For one thing, they are narrow in focus. Magazines are built around very specific areas of interest, and for every interest there is likely to be at least one magazine devoted to it. By the time adolescents are in middle school, they develop strong interests in particular kinds of entertainment, music, sports, etc. Magazines tap into these interests. Teens who love NASCAR racing may say they hate reading, but they will read a magazine about it. And if they will read a magazine about it, they will probably read a book about the sport or a particular driver.

Eight Reasons Why Teens Like Magazines

(Adapted from *Connecting Young Adults and Libraries: A How-To-Do-It Manual* by Patrick Jones)

Capitalizing on Fads—Magazines like *Black Beat*, *Bop*, *Sixteen*, and *Word Up!* focus on popular film, music, and television personalities of the day. "Fanzines" devoted to a particular program, star, or other entity, like *Buffy the Vampire Slayer*, will exploit a craze until its popularity wanes.

Self-Help—Although most teens probably do read magazines for entertainment and recreation, girls in particular also read magazines like *Glamour* and *Seventeen* because they are a great source for advice and information about dating, health issues, relationships, etc.

Social Relevance—Magazines address current events, issues and interests of particular relevance to teens that can spark debate and discussion.

Special Interest—Many magazines cater to a special interests like cars, collectibles, hobbies, professional wrestling, or sports. As teens grow older, they develop special interests, and there may be few books to appeal to those interests. Magazines can fill that void.

Time Commitment—Jones observes that one reason many young adults, particularly boys, do not read books is physical (139). Books require too much time, sitting, and concentration. Magazines can be read quickly—between classes, in the bathroom, on the bus, etc. Readers can also skip an article they are bored with or don't care about. Magazines have great appeal to the short attention spans and increasingly busy schedules of many adolescents.

Universal Interest—Some teens will not read books because they do not want their peers to ostracize them for being brains or nerds. Magazines have more universal appeal among teens, and so do not have the negative stigma attached to reading books.

Visual Appeal—Magazines appealing to teens are heavily laden with photographs and other illustrations. This is particularly appealing to visually oriented teens who like Internet graphics, music videos, and video games.

A large collection of magazines addressing a wide variety of interests is strongly recommended for all libraries. Although the collection is supposed to primarily support the curriculum, it's important for school libraries to have plenty of magazines for recreational reading, too. In public libraries, if you do not have a young adult area, it's best to have magazines with strong teen appeal near where the young adult books are shelved. In classrooms, teachers should have magazines available to read as an option for the sustained silent reading time.

Magazines are high casualty items. They rarely survive more than a few circulations. Some libraries do not circulate magazines at all. Another option is to circulate only past issues, keeping the current one in the library so everyone interested has a chance to see it. If you have a good budget and can afford more than one copy, you could circulate one and keep the other for in-house reading.

Who reads what magazines is very much determined by gender. Fashion/self-help magazines are exclusively geared toward a female audience. That's not to say that boys are not interested in fashion, dating tips, growing up issues, and so on, but there are no magazines for boys that address such issues as there are for girls. There is no teen equivalent of an *Esquire* or *GQ*. Entertainment magazines like *Teen People* are widely read by both genders. Boys are particularly drawn to special interest magazines, such as those dealing with collectibles, games, and sports. Magazines are notorious for going out of business, coming back, and then disappearing again without warning and with great frequency. This is especially true of publications with marginal audiences. The more specialized the focus the more precarious the existence in the world of magazines. This can be a big headache for librarians who have to keep track of many subscriptions and want to be sure they are getting their money's worth. You also have to be aware of the fact that you can have twelve different titles that are virtually interchangeable with one another in content and format. This is particularly the case with entertainment and fashion/self-help magazines. For example, there is no reason to have *Bop*, *J-14*, and *Sixteen*. They all cover the same material. When you are faced with decisions like this, it is most desirable to get feedback from the teens you serve to find out which one they prefer. You can count on them having very definite opinions on the subject.

You must also keep in mind that teenagers always read "older." No seventeen-year-old girl reads *Seventeen*. That magazine has a much younger audience, probably fourteen and younger. A seventeen-year-old reads *Glamour*, *Mademoiselle*, and the adult versions of *Cosmopolitan* and *Vogue*. Do not assume that because a magazine appears to target a particular ethnic or racial group that only that group will read it. A magazine like *The Source*, for example, could be extremely popular with suburban white kids who have helped make rap and hip-hop artists so successful. To judge the appropriateness of a magazine, look at the advertisements in a magazine. Some with strong teen appeal have ads for alcohol and cigarettes. There are also magazines popular with teens that have strong graphic and visual content. *Vibe*, for example, is definitely inappropriate for a middle school library. Depending on the local community standards, it may be okay in a high school or the young adult section of a public library. In any case, teens do read it. Whether you want to give them more direct access to it is a judgment call. Whatever titles you buy for your library, make sure you have a variety that appeal to a wide range of abilities, interests, and tastes.

Works Cited

Jones, Patrick. *Connecting Libraries and Young Adults: A How-To-Do-It Manual.* 2nd ed. New York: Neal-Schuman, 1998.

Magazines with Teen Appeal

Anime (Japanese Animation and Comics)
Animerica
Anime Invasion
Sailor Moon

Collectibles/Genre Favorites/Hobbies
Beckett Baseball Card Monthly
Comics Scene
Dragon (Dungeons and Dragons)
Fangoria (Horror)
Hero Illustrated (Comics)
Scrye: The Guide to Collectible Card Games
Starlog (Science Fiction)
Wizard (Comics)

Cars
Car and Driver
Drag Racer
Hot Rod

Christian
Youthwalk

Entertainment
Black Beat
Bop
Entertainment Weekly
Ignite
J-14
Right On!
Sixteen
Soap Opera Digest
Teen Beat
Teen People
Word Up

Extreme Sports
BMX Action
Thrasher
Transworld BMX
Transworld Motocross
Transworld Skateboarding
Warp

Fashion/Self-Help
Blue Jean
Cosmo Girl
Glamour
Jump
Latina
Mademoiselle
Seventeen
Teen
Teen Vogue
Twist
YM (formerly *Young Miss*)
YSB: Young Sisters and Brother (African-American Focus)

Games
Electronic Gaming Monthly (EGM)
Expert Gamer
Game Informer
Gamepro
Nintendo Power
Play Station
PSM: PS2 & Playstation Magazine

Gay/Lesbian
InsideOUT

Homework Help/Research
Discover
National Geographic World

Humor
MAD
Spy!

Literary
Cicada
Merlyn's Pen
Writes of Passage

Music
Alternative Press
Circus
Guitar Player
Hit Parader
Rolling Stone
Spin

Rap/Hip Hop Music and Culture
The Source
Vibe

Sports
Black Belt (Martial Arts)
Slam (Basketball)
NASCAR Illustrated
NBA Inside Stuff
Sports Illustrated

Wrestling
Pro Wrestling Illustrated
WCW Magazine (World Championship Wrestling)
Wrestle America
WWF Magazine (World Wrestling Federation)

Chapter 8
Resources for Reluctant Readers: Audiobooks

Audiobooks Belong in Classrooms and Libraries

Audiobooks have been around a long time and there is no question that they have been and continue to be enormously popular among many adults. Public libraries of all sizes have at least a small collection of titles. Even Cracker Barrel, a "country cooking" chain of restaurants you can find throughout the United States, has a lending program. It's evident that even adults enjoy being read aloud to. Reading aloud is not just for children.

Yet, it is surprising how little audiobooks are used by teachers in the classroom, especially given the fact that more audiobook versions of children's and young adult titles are available more widely than ever before. Perhaps availability is one reason why teachers do not use them. In my work with New York City public schools, I did not find one school with even a small collection of audiobooks—not even one just restricted to classroom use. Even if such a collection were desirable, acquisitions budgets are too small to justify such purchases. Many school librarians barely have enough money to renew periodical subscriptions and update their encyclopedias. Never mind venturing into a whole new media. Even in a system as large and progressive as the New York Public Library, it is difficult to find in most branches a wide range of audiobook children's and young adult titles. New York Public Library probably has more to choose from than most libraries, but even there they seem to be considered ephemeral material.

If young adult audiobook titles were more accessible in school and public libraries, would teachers be more inclined to use them? Ted Hipple and Elizabeth Goza find that: "Our experience suggests that not many of them [teachers] are even aware that such books exist, an ignorance ironically inconsistent with their appreciation of other media" (364). Among some teachers, there is the belief that listening to an audiobook is not really "reading." Well, it isn't in the traditional sense, but the audiobook does allow students to experience story and all the literary elements they would be exposed to from the actual reading of a text.

Listening to an audiobook is a better alternative than not reading anything at all. Hipple and Gorza note:

> Using audiobooks to introduce students to print literature can be helpful. For many students, reading a book, no matter what it's size, is a daunting task. Some of these students actually hear better than they read; that is they understand what they listen to better than they understand what they read. If they can listen to opening several chapters and, by doing so, can get hooked on the book, the assignment to read on will be a more agreeable one. (366)

Any teacher will agree that helping students develop strong listening skills is as important as developing good reading skills. Audiobooks can do both.

Audiobooks can also bring literature alive to students in a way that cannot be done through their own reading or even through the teacher reading aloud. Professional performers who know how to bring the subtle nuances of a text to life can offer a unique reading experience for students. Barbara Baskin and Karen Harris observe:

> Trained actors who read texts for audiobook recordings, even when their native speech patterns do not reflect those of the books' characters, can simulate local accents, phrasing, emphasis, and other phonological attributes that clearly distinguish various types of speakers. . . . For naïve, limited, or simply inexperienced readers, proper names and uncommon words may be heard correctly pronounced for the first time, offering suitable models, comfortably extending vocabulary, and overcoming possible barriers to the flow of the narrative. Most significantly, the professional narrator, bringing finely honed dramatic skill to an interpretation of the text, can generate excitement and captivate a wide spectrum of listeners from the inept and unwilling to the expert and passionate. (373)

Literature, like poetry and Shakespeare's plays, that is intimidating to any student, but especially to reluctant readers, can be rendered far more appealing in audiobook form. Baskin and Harris note: "Poetry, traditionally a problem for student readers, is presented on tape with expert phrasing, rhythm, accent, and pronunciation as well as sensitivity to mood and tone" (374). Elements in literature like irony, puns, and sarcasm that may be lost on literal-minded students can be brought to life in an audiobook. Baskin and Harris observe:

> Humor may be the most difficult literature for inexpert readers. Timing, emphasis, pause, and stress are as critical to "getting it" as knowledge of vocabulary and allusions. . . . Saracasm, irony, and facetiousness fall flat if read literally, a situation that often happens with students unprepared to decipher wit in what they are reading. (374)

Imagine the deeper appreciation a student can get of Shakespeare's wit if he or she is able to read the text as an actor recites it. Reading can take on a whole new dimension for students when they can discern the lyricism and emotion in a poem.

Why Audiobooks Are Good for Reluctant Readers

In a previous chapter, I noted the significant impact reading aloud can have upon reluctant adolescent readers. Teachers willing to embrace reading aloud as a motivational strategy should be willing embrace audiobooks as well. Beers finds in her research: "The aliterate students I've been interviewing since 1989 have few recollections of being read to aloud" (33). Reading aloud is important in even the secondary grades, as was discussed in an earlier chapter. Beers finds that although the act of the teacher reading a book aloud to her class is indeed desirable, that act does not necessarily address the wide range of abilities and interests one is likely to find in a large classroom setting. She observes:

> For reading aloud to have important effects, it must take place often, over lots of time. Furthermore, the texts must be interesting to the listener, and often they need to be reread. In large classrooms with children who have a wide range of abilities and interests, a teacher might find enough time to read aloud one book in a class period, but not the multiple books that are needed to stimulate the range of students interests. One way around that problem is to use audiobooks in the classroom. (33)

Students can listen to audiobooks in the classroom individually, in the same manner that they would be individually reading a self-selected book during a designated sustained silent reading time. Hipple and

Gorza also advocate the listening of audiobooks among small groups of students who may have a shared interest in a particular author or genre.

Hipple and Gorza note the sense of community that teachers can build among students through the use of audiobooks.

> Audiobooks also facilitate group interactions, something middle school students enjoy, if not demand. Putting six or eight students the tape player and letting them engage in common listening can generate a collegial enjoyment of the text. Literature takes on a communal appeal, much like the stories told round a campfire or passed from generation to generation in pre-print days.(367)

This is particularly important when one considers that peer influence is a major factor in why many adolescents are resistant to reading. There are perceptions among many teens that reading is solitary and antisocial, and that it is something simply "uncool" to do. Using audiobooks in a classroom setting can shatter those perceptions and generate what Hipple and Gorza call "a collegial enjoyment" of reading.

For students who are struggling with reading, audiobooks can also serve as an important bridge to more complex and difficult stories they would not otherwise be willing or able to tackle in print. Beers observes that this use of audiobooks is particularly important with older students:

> The use of audiobooks with struggling, reluctant, or second-language learners is powerful since they act as a scaffold that allows students to read above their actual reading level. This is critical with older students who may still read at a beginner level. While these students must have time to practice reading at their level, they must also have the opportunity to experience the plot structures, themes, and vocabulary of more difficult books.(33)

Audiobooks can make accessible to adolescents texts which they would be unwilling and probably unable to read. The ability to experience these texts in audiobooks form can only build confidence in the reader. Listening to a difficult may make them confident enough to try to actually read more difficult books.

Abridged or Unabridged?

There is debate among librarians and teachers over whether audiobooks made available to young people should be abridged or unabridged. Baskin and Harris favor abbreviated versions of texts. They argue that students "need to be enticed into the world of books, and abridged stories on tape may provide a unique opportunity to do so" (375). They further argue that these abbreviated version, focused almost entirely on plot "require less time and commitment, making them more acceptable to subliterate or aliterate youth" (375). Baskin and Harris take the position that abridged is better than nothing at all. Not all educators, however, agree. Beers advocates buying unabridged recordings. Librarians are likely to take a more purist stance, taking the position of unabridged or nothing.

Both positions are understandable, but which one is preferable for students struggling to read?

Works Cited

Baskin, Barbara H., and Karen Harris. "Heard Any Good Books Lately? The Case for Audiobooks in the Secondary Classroom." *Journal of Reading* 38.5 (February 1995): 372-376.

Beers, Kylene. "Listen While You Read: Struggling Readers and Audiobooks." *School Library Journal* (April 1998): 30-35.

Hipple, Ted, and Elizabeth Goza. "It Ain't Only Books Any More." *Into Focus: Understanding and Creating Middle School Readers.* Eds. Kylene Beers and Barbara G. Samuels. Norwood, MA: Christopher- Gordon, 1998.

Producers of Audiobook Versions of Young Adult Titles

Audio Book Contractors
Box 40115
Washington, D. C. 20016
(202) 363-3429

Audio Bookshelf
74 Prescott Hill Road
Northport, ME 04849
(800) 234-1713
audbkshf@agate.net

BDD Audio
1540 Broadway
New York, NY 10036
(212) 782-9807
www.bdd.com

Blackstone Audio Books
Box 969
Ashland, OR 97520

Chivers Audiobooks
1 Lafayette Road
Box 1450
Hampton, NH 03843
(800) 621-0182

Houghton Mifflin
181 Ballardville St.
Wilmington, MA 01887
(800) 225-3362
www.hmco.com

Listening Library
One Park Avenue
Old Greenwich, CT 06870
(800) 243-5404
moreinfo@listeninglib.com
www.listeninglib.com

Little, Brown
34 Beacon Street
Boston, MA 02108
(800) 759-0190

Live Oak Media
Box 652
West Church Street
Pine Plains, NY 12567
(518) 398-1010

Recorded Books
2700 Skipjack Road
Prince Frederick, MD 20678

(800) 638-1304
www.recordedbks.com

Spoken Arts
Box 100
New Rochelle, NY 10801
(800) 326-4090

Troll Associates
100 Corporate Drive
Mahwah, NJ 07430

Weston Woods (Scholastic, Inc.)
Box 2193
Norwalk, CT 06852
(800) 243-5020
www.scholastic.com

Appendix
Professional Resources

Aliteracy

Beers, Kylene. "Choosing Not to Read: Understanding Why Some Middle Schoolers Just Say No." *Into Focus: Understanding and Creating Middle School Readers.* Eds. Kylene Beers and Barbara G. Samuels. Norwood, MA: Christopher-Gordon, 1998.

————. *Choosing Not to Read: An Ethnographic Study of Seventh-Grade Aliterate Readers.* Unpublished Doctoral Dissertation. University of Houston, 1990.

————. "No Time, No Interest, No Way! Three Voices of Aliteracy." *School Library Journal* (February 1996): 30-33.

————. "No Time, No Interest, No Way! Part 2." *School Library Journal* (March 1996): 110-113.

Chambers, Aidan. *The Reluctant Reader.* Oxford: Pergamon, 1969.

Cope, Jim. "Beyond *Voices of Readers*: Students on School's Effects On Reading." *English Journal* 86.3 (March 1997): 18-23.

Decker, Barbara Cooper. "Aliteracy: What Teachers Can Do to Keep Johnny Reading." *Journal of Teacher Education* 37.6 (November/December 1986): 55-58.

Gentile, Lance, and Merna McMillan. "Why Won't Teenagers Read?" *Journal of Reading* 20.8 (1977): 649-654.

Harding, Margaret. "Where Have All the Children Gone? The Seventh-Grader as Public Library Dropout." *Public Libraries* (Fall 1983): 92-96.

Mikulecky, Larry. *Aliteracy and a Changing View of Reading Goals.* ERIC, 1978. ERIC ED 157 052.

Myers, Walter Dean. "The Reluctant Reader." *Interracial Books for Children Bulletin* 19.3/4 (1989): 14-15.

Ohanian, Susan. "Creating a Generation of Aliterates." *Education Digest* 54.6 (February 1989): 29-32.

Thimmesch, N., ed. *Aliteracy: People Who Can Read But Won't.*Washington, D. C. American Enterprise Institute for Public Policy Reasearch, 1984.

Winkle, Alice. "Research on Aliteracy: Why Johnny Doesn't Read." *Ohio Reading Teacher* 22.2 (1988): 40-47.

Audiobooks

Austin, Patricia, and Karen Harris. "The Audio Argument, or Sound Advice about Literature." *The New Advocate* 12.3 (Summer 1999): 241-247.

Baskin, Barbara H., and Karen Harris. "Heard Any Good Books Lately? The Case for Audiobooks in the Secondary Classroom." *Journal of Reading* 38.5 (February 1995): 372-376.

Beers, Kylene. "Listen While You Read: Struggling Readers and Audiobooks." *School Library Journal* (April 1998): 30-35.

Casbergue, Renee Michelet, and Karen Harris. "Listening and Literacy: Audiobooks in the Reading Program." *Reading Horizons* 37.1 (1996): 48-59.

Diegmuller, K. "Talking Books Pressed into Classroom Service." *Education Week* (May 3, 1995): 6-7.

Harris, Karen H. "Growing Up Listening." *Booklist* 90 (April 15, 1994): 1548.

Hipple, Ted and Elizabeth Goza. "It Ain't Only Books Any More." *Into Focus: Understanding and Creating Middle School Readers.* Eds. Kylene Beers and Barbara G. Samuels. Norwood, MA: Christopher-Gordon, 1998.

Books Appealing to Reluctant Readers

Ammon, Bette D., and Gale W. Sherman. *More Rip-Roaring Reads for Reluctant Young Adult Readers*. Englewood, CO: Libraries Unlimited, 1998.

Baines, Lawrence. "Cool Books for Tough Guys: 50 Books Out of the Mainstream of Adolescent Literature that Will Appeal to Males Who Do Not Enjoy Reading." *The ALAN Review* (Fall 1994): 43-46.

Bodart, Joni Richards. *The World's Best Thin Books: What to Read When Your Book Report Is Due Tomorrow*. Lanham, MD: Scarecrow, 2000.

Jones, Patrick. "Thin Books, Big Problems: Realism and the Reluctant Teen Reader." *The ALAN Review* 21.2 (Winter 1994): 18-28.

Lynn, Barbara A., and Judith A. Druse. "Attention Grabbers for the Reluctant Young Adult Reader." *VOYA: Voice of Youth Advocates* (October 1987): 165-166.

Miller, Frances A. "Books to Read When You Hate to Read: Recommended by Reluctant YA Readers in Grades 7-12." *Booklist* (February 15, 1992): 1100-1101.

Reed, Arthea J. S. *Comics to Classics: A Guide to Books for Teens and Preteens*. New York: Penguin, 1994.

Robb, Laura. "Helping Reluctant Readers Discover Books." *Book Links* (March 1998): 51-53.

Rosenzweig, Sue. "Books that Hooked 'Em: Reluctant Readers Shine as Critics." *American Libraries* (June/July 1996): 74-76.

Sherman, Gale W., and Bette D. Ammon. *Rip-Roaring Reads for Reluctant Teen Readers*. Englewood, CO: Libraries Unlimited, 1993.

Worthy, Jo. "A Matter of Interest: Literature That Hooks Reluctant Readers and Keeps Them Reading." *The Reading Teacher* 50.3 (November 1996): 204-206.

Worthy, Jo, Megan Moorman, and Margo Turner. "What Johnny Likes to Read Is Hard to Find in School." *Reading Research Quarterly* 34.1 (January/February/March 1999): 12-27.

Comics and Graphic Novels

Barker, K. "Graphic Account: The Selection and Promotion of Graphic Novels in Libraries for Young People." *School Librarian* 42.1 (February 1994): 38.

Barron, Daniel D. "Zap! Pow! Wham!: Comics, Graphic Novels, an Education." *School Library Media Activities Monthly* 8 (November 1991): 48-50.

Bruggeman, Lora. "Zap! Whoosh! Kerplow! Building High-Quality Graphic Novel Collections with Impact." *School Library Journal* 43.1 (January 1997): 22-27.

Carraher, Charles E. "Comics: No-nonsense Classroom Aids." *The Science Teacher* 45.11 (November 1975): 30.

"Comic Books for Young Adults." *Booklist* 86 (October 1, 1989): 274-276.

DeCandido, Keith R. A. "Picture This: Graphic Novels in Libraries." *Library Journal* 115.5 (March 15, 1990): 50-55.

Dorrell, Larry D. "Why Comic Books?" *School Library Journal* (November 1987): 30-32.

Dorrell, Larry D., and C. Edward Carroll. "Spiderman at the Library." *School Library Journal* 27.10 (August 1981): 118-120.

Doborwski, Alex. "The Comic Book Is Alive and Well and Living in the History Class." *Social Studies* 67.3 (May/June 1976): 118-120.

Ellman, Neil. "Comics in the Classroom." *Audiovisual Instructor* 24.5 (May 1979): 24-25.

Estes, Sally. "Comics and Graphic Novels for Young Adults." *Booklist* 88 (September 1, 1991): 45.

Freeman, Matt. "The Case for Comics." *Reading Today* 15.3 (December 1997/January 1998): 3-5.

Gagnier, S. Richard. "A Hunger for Heroes." *School Library Journal* (September 1997): 143.

Gibson, M. "Picture This! Snapshots of Work with Graphic Novels, Libraries, and Young Adults." *School Librarian* 46.1 (Spring 1998):14-15.

Goldgell, Rosanne. "Comics as Textbooks." *Instructor* 86.3 (March 1977): 129-130.

Goldsmith, Francisca. "YA Talk: Graphic Novels." *Booklist* 94.17 (May 1, 1998): 1510-1511.

Hipple, Ted and Elizabeth Goza. "It Ain't Only Books Any More." *Into Focus: Understanding and Creating Middle School Readers*. Eds. Kylene Beers and Barbara G. Samuels. Norwood, MA: Christopher-Gordon, 1998.

Jones, Patrick. "Getting Serious about Comics." *VOYA: Voice of Youth Advocates* (April 1988): 15-16.

Kan, Katherine L. "Comics and Graphic Novels in the Library." *VOYA: Voice of Youth Advocates* 22.4 (October 1999): 252-253.

———. "Graphic Novels: A Roundup." *VOYA: Voice of Youth Advocates* 16.6 (February 1994): 359-360.

———. "Graphic Novels, Take Two: A Reaction to 'Creating a Graphic Novel Collection for the Public Library' by Stephen Weiner." *VOYA: Voice of Youth Advocates* (August 1993): 145-146.

———. "Great for Middle School." *VOYA: Voice of Youth Advocates* 24.4 (October 2001): 270-271.

McCloud, Scott. *Understanding Comics: The Invisible Art*. Northampton, MA: Tundra, 1993.

Moore, S. "Comics and Narrative Fiction: The Links." *Assistant Librarian* 90.5 (May 1997): 69-73.

100 Graphic Novels for Public Libraries. Northampton, MA: Kitchen Sink, 1996.

Reid, Calvin. "Picture This." *Publishers Weekly* (October 12, 1990): 17-20.

Rothschild, D. Aviva. *Graphic Novels: A Bibliographic Guide to Book-Length Comics.* Englewood, CO: Libraries Unlimited, 1995.

Sherman, Gale W., and Bette D. Ammon. "Beyond Superman: The Boom in Trade Comics." *School Library Journal* 39 (May 1993): 34-35.

Swain, Emma Halstead. "Using Comic Books to Teach Reading and Language Arts." *Journal of Reading* 22.3 (December 1978): 253-258.

Weiner, Stephen. "Creating a Graphics Novel Collection for the Public Library." *VOYA: Voice of Youth Advocates* 15.5 (December 1992): 269-270, 272.

————. *The 101 Best Graphic Novels.* Ed. Keith R. A. DeCandido. Nantier-Beall-Minoustchine, 2001.

Wright, Gary. "The Comic Book—A Forgotten Medium in the Classroom." *The Reading Teacher* 33.2 (November 1979): 158-161.

High/Low Books

Alvermann, Donna E. "Junior High Basals: Effective Hi/Lo Materials for Remedial High School Readers." *Curriculum Review* 20.5 (November 1981): 442-444.

Carter, Betty, and Richard F. Abrahamson. "The Best of the Hi/Lo Books for Young Adults: A Critical Evaluation." *Journal of Reading* 30.3 (December 1986): 204-211.

Williams, Helen E. "Characterization in High-Interest/Low Vocabulary Level Fiction." *School Library Journal* (February 1987): 31-33.

Impact of Technologies on Reading Habits

Dresang, Eliza T. "Influence of the Digital Environment on Literature for Youth." *Library Trends* 45.4 (Spring 1997): 639-663.

————. *Radical Change: Books for Youth in a Digital Age.* New York: Wilson, 1999.

Dresang, Eliza T., and Kathryn McClelland. "Radical Change: Digital Age Literature and Learning." *Theory Into Practice* 38.3 (Summer 1999): 160-167.

Hipple, Ted, and Elizabeth Goza. "It Ain't Only Books Any More." *Into Focus: Understanding and Creating Middle School Readers.* Eds. Kylene Beers and Barbara G. Samuels. Norwood, MA: Christopher-Gordon, 1998.

Murray, Janet. *Hamlet on the Holodeck: The Future of Narrative in Cyberspace.* New York: Free Press, 1997.

Reinking, David. "Me and My Hypertext: A Multiple Digression Analysis of Technology and Literacy." *The Reading Teacher* 50.8 (May 1997): 626-643.

Skurzynski, Gloria. "It's a Wired World After All: Children, Books, and the Internet." *Theory Into Practice* 38.3 (Summer 1999): 178-183.

Tapscott, Don. *Growing Up Digital: The Rise of the Net Generation.* New York: McGraw-Hill, 1998.

Truett, C. "CD-ROM Storybooks Bring Children's Literature to Life." *Computing Teacher* 21 (August/September 1993): 20-21.

Magazines for Young Adults

Jones, Patrick. "Sex, Thugs, and Rock 'n' Roll: Magazines for Young Adults." *Young Adults and Public Libraries: A Handbook of Materials and Services.* Eds. Mary Anne Nichols and C. Allen Nichols. Westport, CT: Greenwood Press, 1998.

Nonfiction for Young Adults

Abrahamson, Richard F., and Betty Carter. "What We Know about Nonfiction and Young Adult Readers and What We Need to Do about It." *Inspiring Literacy: Literature for Children and Young Adults.* Eds. Sam Sebesta and Ken Donelson. New Brunswick, NJ: Transaction, 1993.

Carter, Betty, and Richard F. Abrahamson. "Castles to Colin Powell: The Truth about Nonfiction." *Into Focus: Understanding and Creating Middle School Readers.* Eds. Kylene Beers and Barbara G. Samuels. Norwood, MA: Christopher-Gordon, 1998.

————. *Nonfiction for Young Adults: From Delight to Wisdom.* Phoenix: Oryx, 1990.

————. "Nonfiction in a Read-Aloud Program." *Journal of Reading* 34.8 (May 1991): 638-642.

————. "Nonfiction—The Teenagers' Reading of Choice, or, Ten Research Studies Every Reading Teacher Should Know." *SIGNAL* 19.2 (1995): 51-56.

————. "Of Survival, School, Wars, and Dreams: Nonfiction that Belongs in English Classes." *English Journal* 76.2 (1987): 104-109.

Colman, Penny. "Nonfiction Is Literature, Too." *The New Advocate* 12.3 (Summer 1999): 215-223.

Kerper, Rick. "Young Adult Non-Fiction: Not Just for Homework Anymore." *Young Adults and Public Libraries: A Handbook of Materials and Services.* Eds. Mary Anne Nichols and C. Allen Nichols. Westport, CT: Greenwood Press, 1998.

Meltzer, Milton. *Nonfiction for the Classroom: Milton Meltzer on Writing, History, and Social Responsibility.* Ed. E. Wendy Saul. New York: Teachers College Press, 1994.

Sullivan, Ed. "Some Teens Prefer It Real: The Case for Young Adult Nonfiction." *English Journal* 90.3 (January 2001): 43-47.

Vanek, Evelyn. "Nonfiction for Reluctant Readers." *Journal of Youth Services in Libraries* 10 (Summer 1997): 426-429.

Picture Books for Young Adults

Aikman, Carol C. "Picture Books and the Secondary Media Specialist." *Indiana Media Journal* 17.1 (Fall 1994): 104-110.

Ammon, Bette D., and Gale Sherman. *Worth a Thousand Words: Picture Books for Older Readers.* Englewood, CO: Libraries Unlimited, 1996.

Benedict, Susan, and Lenore Carlisle, eds. *Beyond Words: Picture Books for Older Readers and Writers.* Portsmouth, NH: Heinemann, 1992.

Hall, Susan. *Using Picture Storybooks to Teach Literary Devices: Recommended Books for Children and Young Adults.* Vol. 1. Phoenix, AZ: Oryx, 1990.

———. *Using Picture Storybooks to Teach Literary Devices: Recommended Books for Children and Young Adults.* Vol. 2. Phoenix, AZ: Oryx, 1994.

Meltzer, Milton. *Nonfiction in the Classroom: Milton Meltzer on Writing, History, and Social Responsibility.* Ed. Wendy Saul. New York: Teachers College Press, 1994.

Miller, Terry. "The Place of Picture Books in Middle-Level Classrooms." *Journal of Adolescent and Adult Literacy* 41.5 (February 1998): 376-381.

Richey, Virginia H., and Kathryn E. Puckett. *Wordless/Almost Wordless Picture Books: A Guide.* Englewood, CO: Libraries Unlimited, 1992.

"Sophisticated Picture Books for the Middle Grades." *Teaching K-8* (May 1994): 54-57.

Reading Aloud

Erickson, Barbara. "Read-Alouds Reluctant Readers Relish." *Journal of Adolescent and Adult Literacy* 40.3 (November 1996): 212-214.

Jennings, J. "You Can't Afford Not to Read Aloud." *Phi Delta Kappan* 71 (1990): 568-569.

Lesene, Teri S. "Reading Aloud to Build Success in Reading." *Into Focus: Understanding and Creating Middle School Readers.* Eds. Kylene Beers and Barbara G. Samuels. Norwood, MA: Christopher-Gordon, 1998.

Trelease, Jim. "Jim Trelease Speaks on Reading Aloud to Children." *The Reading Teacher* 43.3 (December 1989): 200-207.

Zientarski, Deborah Phelps, and Donald D. Pottorff. "Reading Aloud to Low Achieving Secondary Students." *Reading Horizons* 35.1 (1994): 44-51.

Reading Attitudes and Habits of Young Adults

Alexander, J. E., and R. C. Filler. *Attitudes and Reading.* Newark, DE: International Reading Association, 1976.

Anderson, R. C., P. T. Wilson, and L. G. Fielding. "Growth in Reading and How Children Spend Their Time Outside of School." *Reading Research Quarterly* 23.3 (1988): 285-303.

Beers, G. Kylene. *Middle School Avid Readers Talk about Reading: An Ethnographic Account.* Unpublished Manuscript. University of Houston, 1988.

Briggs, L. D. "Motivation: A Problem Area in Reading." *Reading Improvement* 233 (1986): 2-6.

Bruckerhoff, C. "What Do Students Say about Reading Instruction?" *The Clearing House* 51 (1977): 104-107.

Carlsen, G. Robert. *Books and the Teen-Age Reader: A Guide for Teachers, Librarians and Parents.* New York: Bantam, 1971.

Carlsen, G. Robert, and Anne Sherrill. *Voices of Readers: How We Come to Love Books.* Urbana, IL: National Council of Teachers of English, 1988.

Collins, Kimberly Leanne. "Litanies of a Literature Lover, or Confessions of a Young Adult Reader." *Mosaics of Meaning:*

Enhancing the Intellectual Life of Young Adults through Story. Ed. Kay E. Vandergrift. Lanham, MD: Scarecrow, 1996.

Cope, Jim. "Beyond Voices of Readers: Students on School's Effects On Reading." *English Journal* 86.3 (March 1997): 18-23.

Early, Margaret. "Stages of Growth in Literary Appreciation." *English Journal* 49.3 (March 1960): 161-167.

Frasher, S. R. "Know Your Reluctant Reader's Interests." *Reading World* 18.1 (1978): 67-71.

Gallo, Donald R. "Reactions to Required Reading: Some Implications from a Study of Connecticut." *Connecticut English Journal* 15.2 (1984): 7-11.

Gentile, Lance, and Merna McMillan. "Why Won't Teenagers Read?" *Journal of Reading* (1997): 649-654.

Greaney, V. "Factors Related to Amount and Type of Leisure Time Reading." *Reading Research Quarterly* 15.3 (1980): 336-357.

Hansen, H. S. "The Impact of the Home Literary Environment on Reading Attitudes." *Elementary English* 46 (1969): 17-24.

Heathington, B. and J. Alexander. "Do Classroom Teachers Emphasize Attitudes Toward Reading?" *Journal of Reading* 22.8 (1979): 709-713.

Isakson, Marne B. "Learning about Reluctant Readers through Their Letters." *Journal of Reading* 34.8 (May 1991): 632-637.

Johnston, P., and P. Winograd. "Passive Failure in Reading." *Journal of Reading Behavior* 17 (1985): 279-300.

"Kids Closing the Book on Reading for Fun." *Wichita Eagle* (September 24, 1995): 16A.

Krogness, Mary Mercer. *Just Teach Me, Mrs. K: Talking, Reading, and Writing with Resistant Adolescent Learners.* Portsmouth, NH: Heinemann, 1995.

Lancy, David F., and Bernard L. Hayes. "Interactive Fiction and the Reluctant Reader." *English Journal* 77.7 (November 1988): 42-46.

Livaudais, M. *A Survey of Secondary Students' Attitudes Toward Reading Motivational Activities.* Unpublished Doctoral Dissertation. University of Houston, 1985.

Lowery-Moore, Hollis. "Voices of Middle School Readers." *Into Focus: Understanding and Creating Middle School Readers.* Eds. Kylene Beers and Barbara G. Samuels. Norwood, MA: Christopher-Gordon, 1998.

Mellon, C. "Teenagers Do Read: What Rural Youth Say about Leisure Reading." *School Library Journal* 33.6 (1987): 27-30.

Moon, C. and C. G. Wells. "The Influence of the Home on Learning to Read." *Journal of Research in Reading* 2 (1979): 53-62.

Morrow, L. "Attitudes of Teachers, Principals, and Parents Toward Promoting Voluntary Reading in the Elementary Schools." *Reading Research and Instruction* 25 (1986): 116-130.

Mueller, D. L. "Teacher Attitudes Toward Reading." *Journal of Reading* 17.4 (1973): 202-205.

O'Rourke, W. "Are Parents an Influence on Adolescent Reading Habits?" *Journal of Reading* 22.4 (1979): 340-343.

Rosenblatt, Louise. *The Reader, the Text, the Poem: The Transactional Theory of the Literary Work.* Carbondale, IL: Southern Illinois University Press, 1978.

Smith, Frank. *Understanding Reading: A Psycholinguistic Analysis of Reading and Learning to Read.* Hillsdale, NJ: Erlbaum, 1988.

Teale, William H. "Assessing Attitudes Toward Reading: Why and How." *Motivating Children and Young Adults to Read.* Eds. James L. Thomas and Ruth M. Loring. Phoenix, AZ: Oryx, 1979.

Troy, A. "Motivation and the Adolescent Reader." *Reading Horizons* 22.4 (1982): 247-252.

Wood, L. "Teenagers' Reading Habits." *Publishers Weekly* 234.5 (1988): 132.

Series Books for Young Adults

Makowski, Silk. "Serious about Series: Selection Criteria for a Neglected Genre." *VOYA: Voice of Youth Advocates* 16.6 (February 1994): 349-351.

Reid, Louann, and Ruth K. J. Cline. "Our Repressed Reading Addictions: Teachers and Young Adult Series Books." *English Journal* 86.3 (March 1997): 68-70.

Ross, Catherine Sheldrick. "If They Read Nancy Drew, So What? Series Book Readers Talk Back." *Library and Information Science Review* 17 (1995): 201-236.

Sparanese, Ann. "R. L. Stine Meets Horatio Alger: Quality Versus Popularity in the Young Adult Collection." *Young Adults and Public Libraries: A Handbook of Materials and Services.* Eds. Mary Anne Nichols and C. Allen Nichols. Westport, CT: Greenwood Press, 1998.

Strategies for Reaching Reluctant Readers

Allen, J. *It's Never Too Late: Leading Adolescents to Lifelong Literacy.* Portsmouth, NH: Heinemann, 1995.

Beers, Kylene, and Barbara G. Samuels, Eds. *Into Focus: Understanding and Creating Middle School Readers.* Norwood, MA: Christopher-Gordon, 1998.

Casteel, Clifton A. "Motivating Reluctant Readers to Become Mature Readers." *Reading Improvement* 26.2 (Summer 1989): 98-102.

Caswell, Linda J., and Nell K. Duke. "Non-Narrative as a Catalyst for Literacy Development." *Language Arts* 75.2 (February 1998): 108-117.

Ciani, A. J., ed. *Motivating Reluctant Readers.* Newark, DE: International Reading Association, 1981.

Clary, Linda Mixon. "Getting Adolescents to Read." *Journal of Reading* 34 (February 1991): 340-345.

Cone, J. "Appearing Acts: Creating Readers in a High School English Class." *Harvard Educational Review* 64: 450-473.

Conlon, Alice. "Unleashing the Power of Reading in Your School and Library." *Catholic Library World* (December 1995): 22-23.

Cooper, Cathie E. "Thirteen Ways to Promote Books." *Book Report* 10 (January/February 1992): 19-20.

Criscuolo, N. "Reading Motivation through the Teacher-Parent Partnership." *Motivating Children and Young Adults to Read 2.* Eds. J. L. Thomas and R. M. Loring. Phoenix, AZ: Oryx, 1983.

Cullinan, Bernice E. *Read to Me: Raising Kids Who Love to Read.* New York: Scholastic, 1992.

Culliton, T. "Techniques for Developing Reading Interests and Attitudes." *Reading in the Middle School: Perspectives in Reading, No. 18.* Ed. G. Duffy. Newark, DE: International Reading Association, 1974.

Daniel, Patricia L. "A Celebration of Literacy: Nine Reluctant Students and One Determined Teacher." *Language Arts* 73.6 (October 1996): 420-428.

Davidson, Judith, and David Koppenhaver. *Adolescent Literacy: What Works and Why.* 2nd ed. New York: Garland, 1993.

Decker, Barbara Cooper. "Aliteracy: What Teachers Can Do to Keep Johnny Reading." *Journal of Teacher Education* 37.6 (November/December 1986): 55-58.

Duffy, G. ed. *Reading in the Middle School: Perspectives in Reading, No. 18.* Newark, DE: International Reading Association, 1974.

Edmonds, Leslie. "Selling Reading: Library Service to Reluctant Adolescent Readers." *Illinois Libraries* (June 1986): 374-377.

Farnan, Nancy. "Connecting Adolescents and Reading: Goals at the Middle Level." *Journal of Adolescent and Adult Literacy* (March 1996): 436-445.

Frasher, R. S. "Know Your Reluctant Reader's Interests." *Reading World* 18.1 (1978): 67-71.

Fredericks, Anthony D. "Developing Positive Reading Attitudes." *The Reading Teacher* 36.2 (1982): 38-40.

Gallo, Donald R. "Short Stories—Long Overdue." *Into Focus: Understanding and Creating Middle School Readers*. Eds. Kylene Beers and Barbara G. Samuels. Norwood, MA: Christopher-Gordon, 1998.

Gaskins, Irene W. "There's More to Teaching At-Risk and Delayed Readers than Good Reading Instruction." *The Reading Teacher* 51.7 (April 1998): 534-547.

Greaney, V. "Factors Related to Amount and Type of Leisure Time Reading." *Reading Research Quarterly* 15.3 (1980): 336-357.

Grimes, Marijo. "Finding Hooks to Catch Reluctant Readers." *English Journal* (January 1991): 45-47.

Hansen, Joyce. "Needed: Quality Literature for Reluctant Readers." *Interracial Books for Children* 15.4 (1984): 9-11.

Hasbrouck, Ellen Kidd. "Sparking Young Adult Reading." *Emergency Librarian* 14.2 (November/December 1986): 13.

Helmstetter, A. "Year-Long Motivation in the 8th Grade 'Reluctant' Class." *Journal of Reading* 31.3 (1987): 244-247.

Hinchman, W. S. "Reading Clubs Instead of Literature Classes." *English Journal* 6.2 (February 1917): 88-95.

Holbrook, Hilary. "Motivating Reluctant Readers: A Gentle Push." *Motivating Children and Young Adults to Read*. Eds. James L. Thomas, and Ruth M. Loring. Phoenix, AZ: Oryx, 1983.

Huck, Charlotte. "Strategies for Improving Interest and Appreciation in Literature." *Elementary Reading Instructions: Selected Materials.* 2nd ed. A. Beery, ed. Boston: Allyn and Bacon, 1983.

Hunt, Gladys M., and Barbara Hampton. *Read for Your Life: Turning Teens Into Readers.* Grand Rapids, MI: Zondervan, 1992.

Ivey, Gay. "Reflections on Teaching Struggling Middle School Readers." *Journal of Adolescent and Adult Literacy* 42.5 (February 1999): 372-381.

Johns, J. L., and L. Lunt. "Motivating Reading: Professional Ideas." *The Reading Teacher* 28.8 (1975): 617-619.

Kahn, N. B. "A Proposal for Motivating More Students to Lifetime Reading of Literature." *English Journal* 63.2 (1974): 34-43.

Knowles, Elizabeth, and Martha Smith. *Reading Rules! Motivating Teens to Read.* Englewood, CO: Libraries Unlimited, 2001.

Krashen, Stephen. *The Power of Reading: Insights from the Research.* Englewood, CO: Libraries Unlimited, 1993.

Labbo, L., and William Teale. "Cross-Age Reading: A Strategy for Helping Poor Readers." *The Reading Teacher* 43.6 (1990): 362-369.

Lenox, Mary F. "The Reluctant Adolescent Reader: Action Steps for Librarians." *Catholic Library World* 55.8 (1984): 352-354.

Leonhardt, Mary. *Keeping Kids Reading: How to Raise Avid Readers in the Video Age.* New York: Crown, 1996.

———. "Make Lemonade: How to Sweeten Your School's Climate for Reading." *School Library Journal* 44.11 (November 1998): 28-31.

———. *Parents Who Love Reading, Kids Who Don't: How It Happens and What You Can Do About It.* New York: Crown, 1993.

Lesene, Teri S. "Developing Lifetime Readers: Suggestions from Fifty Years of Research." *English Journal* (October 1991): 61-64.

Lesene, Teri S., Lois Buckman, Cathy Caves, and Bonnie Day. "Reaching Reluctant Readers: The Student Teacher Online Mentoring Project." *The ALAN Review* 24.2 (Winter 1997): 31-35.

Mackey, Margaret, and Ingrid Johnston. "The Book Resisters: Ways of Approaching Reluctant Teenage Readers." *School Libraries Worldwide* 2.1 (January 1996): 25-38.

Matthews, C. E. "Lap Reading for Teenagers." *Journal of Reading* 30 (1987): 480-485.

McTeague, Frank. *Shared Reading in the Middle and High School Years*. Portsmouth, NH: Pembroke/Heinemann, 1992.

Moniuszko, Linda K. "Motivation: Reaching Reluctant Readers Age 14-17." *Journal of Reading* (September 1992): 32-34.

Morrow, L. M. "Developing Young Voluntary Readers: The Home-the Child-the School." *Reading Research and Instruction* 25.1 (Fall 1985): 1-8.

Morton, Kay, and Mary Forer. "The Big Easy." *School Library Journal* 45.2 (February 1999): 47.

Nell, Victor. *Lost in a Book: The Psychology of Reading for Pleasure*. New Haven, CT: Yale University Press, 1988.

Nussbaum, Marilyn. "An Attempt to Meet the Needs of the Reluctant Reader." *Ohio Media Spectrum* 32.1 (1980): 30-31.

Oldfather, Penny. "What's Needed to Maintain and Extend Motivation for Literacy in the Middle Grades." *Journal of Reading* (March 1995): 420-422.

Parcell, Kit. "REACHing for Books: Promoting Lesiure Reading at the High School Level." *Indiana Media Journal* (Fall 1993): 15-18.

Perez, Samuel A. "Children See, Children Do: Teachers as Reading Models." *The Reading Teacher* 40.1 (October 1986): 8-11.

Podl, Jody Brown. "Introducing Teens to the Pleasures of Reading." *Educational Leadership* 53.1 (September 1995): 56-57.

Raban, Elana. "Reaching the Able but Unwilling Reader." *School Library Journal* 27.4 (December 1980): 37.

Ramos, Francisco, and Stephen Krashen. "The Impact of One Trip to the Public Library: Making Books Available May Be the Best Incentive for Reading." *The Reading Teacher* 51.7 (April 1998): 614-615.

Rasinski, Timothy V. "Inertia and Reading: Stimulating Interest in Books and Reading." *Middle School Journal* (May 1991): 30-33.

Sanacore, Joseph. "Encouraging the Lifetime Reading Habit." *Journal of Reading* (March 1992): 474-477.

Sebesta, Sam, and Ken Doneslon, eds. *Inspiring Literacy: Literature for Children and Young Adults*. New Brunswick, NJ: Transaction, 1993.

Shuman, R. "Reading with a Purpose: Strategies to Interest Reluctant Readers." *Journal of Reading* 25.8 (1982): 725-730.

Smith, Frank. *Understanding Reading: A Psycholinguistic Analysis of Reading and Learning to Read*. Hillsdale, NJ: Erlbaum, 1988.

Storey, D. C. "Reading Role Models: Fictional Readers in Children's Books." *Reading Horizons* 26 (1986): 140-148.

Sullivan, J. L. *An Antidote for Aliteracy: Aliteracy—People Who Can Read but Won't*. ERIC Document EDRS No. ED 255 934.

Thomas, James L., and Ruth M. Loring, eds. *Motivating Children and Young Adults to Read*. 2nd ed. Phoenix, AZ: Oryx, 1983.

Treu, Carol Evans. "Luring Readers Out of Hiding." *Voices from the Middle* 2.2 (April 1995): 29-40.

Turner, Gwendolyn Y. *"Motivating Reluctant Readers: What Can Educators Do?" Reading Improvement* (Spring 1992): 50-55.

Turner, Pat W. "Wrestling with Reluctant Readers." *School Library Journal* (December 1994): 42.

U. S. Department of Education. *What Works: Research about Teaching and Learning.* Washington, D. C.: United States Department of Education, 1986.

Van Jura, Sarah A. "Secondary Students at Risk: Two Giant Steps Toward Independence in Reading." *Journal of Reading* 27.6 (March 1984): 540-543.

Wilhelm, Jeffrey D. "Reading is Seeing: Using Visual Response to Improve the Literary Reading of Reluctant Readers." *Journal of Reading Behavior* 27.4 (December 1995): 467-503.

Winograd, P. and S. Paris. "A Cognitive and Motivational Agenda for Reading Instruction." *Educational Leadership* 46 (December 1988/ January 1989): 30-36.

Worthy, Jo. "Removing Barriers to Voluntary Reading for Reluctant Readers: The Role of School and Classroom Libraries." *Language Arts* 73.7 (November 1996): 483-492.

Worthy, Jo, Margo Turner, and Megan Moorman. "The Precarious Place of Self-Selected Reading." *Language Arts* 75.4 (April 1998): 296-303.

Using Young Adult Literature in the Classroom

Bushman, John H. "Young Adult Literature in the Classroom—Or Is It?" *English Journal* 86.3 (March 1997): 35-40.

Carter, Candy, and Zora Rashkis, eds. *Ideas for Teaching English in the Junior High and Middle School.* Urbana, IL: National Council of Teachers of English, 1980.

Brown, J. E., and E. C. Stephens. *Teaching Young Adult Literature: Sharing the Connection.* Belmont, CA: Wadsworth, 1995.

Herz, Sarah K., and Donald R. Gallo. *From Hinton to Hamlet: Building Bridges Between Young Adult Literature and the Classics.* Westport, CT: Greenwood, 1996.

Monseau, Virginia R., and Gary M. Salvner, eds. *Reading Their World: The Young Adult Novel in the Classroom.* Portsmouth, NH: Boynton Cook/Heinemann, 1992.

Reed, Arthea J. S. *Reaching Adolescents: The Young Adult Book and the School*. New York: Macmillan, 1994.

Samuels, Barbara G. "Creating Lifetime Readers: A Novel Idea." *Into Focus: Understanding and Creating Middle School Readers*. Eds. Kylene Beers and Barbara G. Samuels. Norwood, MA: Christopher-Gordon, 1998.

Small, Robert C. "The Junior Novel and the Art of Literature." *English Journal* 66 (October 1977): 55-59.

Stover, Lois Thomas. *Young Adult Literature: The Heart of the Middle School Curriculum*. Portsmouth, NH: Boynton Cook/Heinemann, 1996.

Worthy, Jo, Megan Moorman, and Margo Turner. "What Johnny Likes to Read Is Hard to Find in School." *Reading Research Quarterly* 34.1 (January/February/March 1999): 12-27.

Index

About the Author

Edward T. Sullivan received his B.A. in English from Glassboro State College, an M.A. in English literature from Memphis State University, and a M.S. in library and information sciences from the University of Tennessee, Knoxville. He has worked as a youth specialist for the New York Public Library and as a library director for the Children's Defense Fund. He currently works as a library media specialist in Jefferson County, Tennessee and as an adjunct instructor, for the University of Tennessee School of Information Sciences. This is his second book for Scarecrow Press. *The Holocaust in Literature for Youth: A Guide and Resource Book*, published in 1999, received unanimous acclaim in several professional journal reviews. He is also the author of over one hundred articles, bibliographies, and reviews for such journals as *The Book Report*, *English Journal*, *Multicultural Review*, *The New Advocate*, *School Library Journal*, and *VOYA*. He lives in Oak Ridge, Tennessee, with his wife Judy and their three cats.